THE FORGOTTEN SACRED ESSENCE: AN OFFERING TO HUMANITY

ABHINAND.T

Made with ❤ on the Notion Press Platform
www.notionpress.com

In Loving Memory of My Father

My whole writing career belongs to my dear father; who had worked hard for decades, earned all he could without even spent the slightest of it on his own needs. He did all of that for the betterment of our family. It is from that preciously kept little wealth; I mustered the power to become a writer. With very few people to motivate and had known about the non-profit style this career offered to its newest members, I wrote five books with a total of over four hundred thousand words, all because of my father's invisible presence, and from the blessings offered by the soul of the Universe.

Contents

Preface

"A good book can bring a lot of changes to a person's life". A few years ago, this statement invoked no thought in me. What can a single book do? I thought. Out of all the entertainment activities, reading is not an easy task; it requires concentration and demands a peaceful mind. Then why would anyone opt to read fiction books, especially when people have a lot of difficult exam related books to cover. I did have such kind of thoughts. After graduation, I opted to study English literature for my post-graduation and, it changed my thoughts.

Art is for Art's own sake, Art is solely for entertainment purposes, and I do agree with that. But books are not solely for entertainment. It is through books, we get to more understand a character and, their emotions, their struggles. This understanding stirs our thoughts, and we will try to find the answers, this process enhances our mind. The things that I have said, am speaking from my own experience as a reader. The problems, struggles, lack of understanding I had, more importantly my perspective on; what is life and its purpose, all of these changed from reading books.

The problems faced by each generation of people, are different. Thus, it is a book's objective to show its readers about the issues faced by humanity, of their respective generation. Even though no good solution is to be offered, it is important to show them the kind of troubles they would be confronting in their future. Books are the perfect choice for such a mission.

Out of all my works, writing this book was the easiest. I was like a medium for one mysterious power that took birth in me, when I was writing the final part of the Pillscape Trilogy. And it was that mystery power which commanded me to write this book in both English and Malayalam language.

During the time I was writing this book, I felt like a student who was carefully writing down the notes spoken out loud by the teacher.

About The Author

Abhinand.T (born November 7, 1999, Kerala) a newly risen Indian novelist, known for his science-fiction trilogy of novels called **The Pillscape Trilogy** published in the year **2024**, which includes, *'The Accidental Ventures of Kiran'* *'The Damaged Pickup Truckerar'* and *'The Flambopian Escapade'*. The whole trilogy discusses the hypothetical situation that if we human beings were some puppets of one massive invisible force ready to conduct one merciless mission on the entire Universe! And what if this force possessed magical powers, and had control over scientific knowledge, time, consciousness, nature etc. His other works include the Philosophical drama *"The Forgotten Sacred Essence: An offering to Humanity"* and the Horror drama *"The Garlic farm Graveyard is Not the Reason!"* both published in Malayalam and English language, in the year 2025.

The second son of Mr Thulasi C and Mrs Sudha, has an elder brother AravindT. Abhinand earned his graduate degree in Malayalam literature, and his post graduate degree in English literature, both from Kerala University. He successfully achieved the certificate of UGC NET in English literature, which is an exam conducted in India to determine the qualification for Assistant professor in Indian universities and colleges.

He is passionate about writing, which encouraged him to become a full-time writer, specialized in existential philosophy. He is against the Alienation, Escapism and Selfishness widespread across the post-modern world, a major theme of his writings.

ONE

BEGINNING

(Intense snoring followed by a loud scream) What the hell! Who turned on the light and why I can't switch it off?

"Greetings Author. It is me, the Soul of Fiction" Bright light spoke.

Sorry Soul, continue,

"I know you have decided to stop your writing career to focus more on your job career, and you are having long peaceful sleep for weeks" Bright light Spoke.

Yes indeed. Writing Fiction is difficult, and you know how much mentally exhausted I was at the time of writing. And yes, I am currently working as an editor and content writer, and it feels great to earn good, work less. Finally! Ooh, I am excited about my life right now.

"Bad news. I want you to create a new book, non-fiction, to explain about the problems this world is struggling with, and you should provide philosophical solutions to most of them. I know you have answers to my concerns. Your new project starts now, get up and create the grandest plot you have ever created. And don't worry about narrating the work, I will arrange a narrator for you, just put your good mind into this project" Bright light replied.

Can't I have a good peaceful life like other people. You know how much I suffered in the past, have I no opportunity to make up for all that? Please, leave me alone, find another writer, am sure there are a lot of writers capable of doing what you want me to do

"No, you must do this. I am not asking you help! And for your information, I believe in you. Yes, there are people more talented than you. But I know you possess great knowledge about yourself, and you are at your peak age. And I did help you in your last work. Now, stop talking, get ready, and don't forget to include this conversation of us, it will provide an intro for the readers" Bright light replied.

(silence)

Ok, I will do it for you, Soul of Fiction. But you must enlighten me more about what you really want me to do. What kind of philosophy context are you talking about? And I must add, there exists many philosophical books already, wouldn't that be enough?

"No! I don't know how to answer your question either. You see, I know there exists these kinds of book, but I have been told by someone who is higher than me, to advise you to create this work, and if you don't, your creative talent shall be taken back by me, as advised by the 'someone' and please don't ask who is this 'someone' now stop wasting time, start writing" Bright light spoke.

(silence)

With all due respect... Stop pushing me, it takes time. And I strongly believe that I don't possess the legitimate philosophical knowledge. Yes, I do think on an amateur level, but writing a whole book on such a matter needs more knowledge.

"You don't have to write a bulky book, and don't worry about getting stuck on thoughts, even if you do get stuck, close your eyes and calm your mind, you will find what you need" Bright light replied.

Ok. I am going to start...

TWO
SECOND BEGINNING

(heavy breathing) Whoa! Where am I? What is happening? Darkness all around me. Please don't tell me this is another work of his. Am too tired from narrating the last work of his, have some mercy, will you? Oh, what is that? It is the bright light, the Almighty of Fiction! Please, save me lord...

"Greetings mister Narrator, I am very honoured to tell you that you have done a great job in narrating your previous work. And I want you to narrate this short book for me" The bright light spoke.

With all due respect. Can't I have a little rest? Am much exhausted. Please tell the Author to narrate this one himself. He is talented, isn't he? Why bother me?

"This isn't about narrating a fictional fantasy story; it is much more than that. You will be narrating a non-fiction work. And if it comforts you, I will be your mentor for this work" Bright light replied.

Oh, that is a relief for sure. Am feeling well. If you don't mind me asking, what is this new book about? How to become a billionaire at twenty? How to make women fall in love with? How to be successful in life? How to efficiently cheat others?

"No! This has nothing to do with the materialist aspects of the world; it is a philosophical work. I know you are terrified, but you don't have to worry a lot thinking about what to do. Time will guide you, wait here" Bright light replied and disappeared.

Oh no! What have I done! I should not have done a good job at narrating my final work. Am completely trapped, I don't know what to do with philosophy, am only good at fantasy blunders. Lord, spare me, choose another narrator. What about the Author? he has some high standard certificates up his sleeves; guess he is good at philosophical way of narration than me. Please let me out of this.

"No, you should narrate this work, don't beg anymore. I have already mentioned your passive presence, stop overreacting, start narrating. Best wishes" Bright light came, replied, disappeared.

(silence)

I have been standing in darkness for over an hour now! What is happening to me? Am I going to be stuck here forever? Was that bright light not the Almighty of Fiction? Am I ordered to describe the philosophy of darkness? You know, the world is nothing but a Nothing. Yes, such philosophical thoughts do exist, weird but true. Oh, something's happening! I can see a large playground, an open auditorium, a big building with a lot of windows, a white colour bus covered in strip lights humming inside the auditorium. Oh, there are people crowding near the bus, mostly teens probably students. This is a college, and these students are entering the bus, college tour. In addition to the twenty-two students, there are six adults, four parents, two teaching staffs, one male, one female.

The male teacher takes attendance, gets everyone inside the bus, blows a whistle, the bus takes off. This is supposed to be a philosophical work, isn't it? Yes, I do believe the bright light mentioned it. Oh no, maybe I was spawned in a different spot. Almighty of Fiction, help me...

"Boy, stop overthinking. Just follow the bus!" someone whispered in my ears. Ok, whatever... I have been following the bus for over four hours now; it never stopped once! And finally, the bus made its first stop at the front of a shop building. 'Cheapstaurant' the board says, ok, they have started ransacking the place, more gluttonous than ever. Some of the boys stuffed two chicken legs in their mouth at once. What is this? Competition? The four parents, not better either, they are eating like it is their last meal. Oh... I should describe about Gluttony, shouldn't I? I mean, Gluttony is indeed a deadly sin, philosophy? Oh no! I don't know how to elaborate. Why people choose me to do this kind of stuff! Am only good at hiding my whole existence behind a creepy old desk.

Anyway... Gluttony is injurious, dear readers. And you will gain unwanted weight all over your body, turning yourself into a bag of potato, the metaphorical one... That was bad, guess I should not get into these kinds of high knowledge matters. (silence) Ok, they have finished their fooding, enter the bus, off we go... The second stop has arrived, a forest. Oh man, am getting some nostalgia from the previous work I have narrated. What the hell was that! the freaking rainbow deer! The rotten fruit massacre! (silence) The tour group entered the forest after buying tickets. The driver sits alone inside the bus, and why is he staring at my direction, Am I not invisible?

I did an absurd action with my lower body, but none of the passerby people noticed me. The driver finally called me to join his driver cabin, I flew inside the bus,

Driver: 'Why stay here? Follow them'

Me: 'You can see me? How? Please don't answer you have eyes'

Driver: (laughs) 'Am not one of them, am just a helper, a helping hand to move the story forward'

Me: 'Oh, can you please explain about different philosophy ideas, thoughts, and add some points on Gluttonous Sin?'

Driver: 'Calm yourself boy, stop worrying about such matters, you are just the narrator. If it comforts you, from the start to this moment, you have done a great job narrating. But you staying here like a dumbass hurts me, go there and cover the characters. Stop worrying about difficult matters, when the time comes, all your confusions will be cleared. Have fun narrating'

I went inside the forest; the tour group is in a meeting under an umbrella shaped tree. Come on teachers, let your students have some rest! Oh, they are not lecturing but sharing their college time experience, can already see some unhappy faces. The teachers are praising the class, the best class they worked with, good students ever, should find success, be classmates forever, be kind and happy... I am getting tired!

The parents are given the opportunity to deliver their speeches as well. Again, the clichéd stuff popped up, study hard, marry fast, get a job as soon as possible, never waste time doing unwanted things... What is this? Is this the philosophy discussion am supposed to narrate?

The students have started their farewell speeches,

: I don't know what to say... I can't believe that we are getting near the end of our campus life. Time does travel faster (cries) I want this classroom life to be endless, I propose all of us to swear an oath to meet somewhere every year, friends forever (cries)

(claps, cheers, screams filled the air)

: I am speechless, I have no idea about making a speech. I will try my best... I am getting burdened with the sweet memories we had together, the times we skipped classes to see movies, ate delicious foods together, played like little toddlers at the park, romance at the beach-

He just went too far. The parents started bickering about his last comment, luckily, the male teacher calmed the situation by explaining that the students are just speaking out the made-up scripts folded in their sleeves. Nothing to worry. The parents are calmed. The students' farewell speeches continue.

: It was a great campus life, am happy to be part of this class. I made few friends from here, and a whole lot of memories and wisdom. If we were to meet in the bright distant future, I would buy them a drink for cheers.

(crowd boos, someone comments 'who the freak is you, get lost!')

Once again, the parents are irritated, start to curse the students for making bad comments. The students boo the parents, someone made a loud comment "Get lost Grandpas, odd one outside!" Parents are enraged again; they made their way back to the Bus. (crowd cheers)

: Calm down friends, I have a huge announcement to make (crowd chants 'what') You guys already know that I am not well made to grasp the easiest of equations and have attended only a very few classes (crowd chants 'Hell yaa') But you all believe in my bigger heart (crowd chants 'Yes') And this heart is filled with my unconditional love for you, Cecily. I love you... (crowd chants Yes Yes Yes...)

The whole class plus the speaker's eyes are staring at a girl, sitting behind all the students. She angrily replied "NO". The boy is heartbroken; he leaves the stage and slowly walks back to the bus meanwhile the crowd boos him...

Ok, enough of this childish drama. What am I supposed to do? Am getting exhausted narrating this piece of irrelevant talks. Am I supposed to comment on these replies? Ok, let me try... No, I can't do it. Help!

(silence)

No, I don't want silence. Ok, here is what am going to do from now on. Am stopping my narration of this pathetic teenage mockery. Will only narrate the journey, and other important matters that does not include absurd chattering's.

Ok, they all went back to the bus, and made way to a snowy place. The parents have no interest in going to this new destination. What happened was that they were planned to go to the Alice Island, which is an island created by humans, in the style of medieval fantasy. But the driver informed them about the route blockage to that place and suggested them to agree to go to the snowy mountain, not too far away. Students were thrilled to scream a big Yes. The students mocked the parents for being cowards, and it made their ego hurt, thus they agreed to the plan, still they look angry. The driver has finally decided to end this dramatic childish nonsense by increasing the music volume, thank you Sir...

The snowy mountain has arrived; freezing gusts penetrated the bus through the little openings. The cold breeze plus the parent's curse words plus the students scream made the bus not habitable. Glad am just flying above them like a ghost. The narrow-curved roads, bumpy, filled with melted ice water, and the sharp ice glacier walls standing on both sides, staring at the bus constantly. Am feeling it's time to end this introduction part, am getting Goosebumps, have I ever thought of getting inside a non-fiction philosophical book? Never. And the absence of the author controlling me is a big relief...

The whole place is covered in fog, can barely see the bus that is now making its way to a snowy mountain, but has good condition roads, yet narrow. And the bus is approaching a dead end soon because of the fallen ice rocks... The driver took a sharp turn! the time has come. Rest in bottles, dear characters. Goodbye... (Blimpppp) The bus stooped into the hard snowy ground, half submerged. Screams bursted out of the bus. Nine students, four parents, both the teachers, survived the crash. They are scared, and a few are crying. I entered the bus, the casualties are not inside, they must have disappeared and spawned inside their respective bottles.

Aaaah my vision! Stop torching my eyes. "Mister narrator, I want you to explain the bottle metaphor you are using repeatedly now. I know what it is, let the readers know it" Bright light spoke.

What! Why do I have to explain it? with all due respect. I strongly believe I have described it in the previous book I have narrated, to be precise, the final part of the Trilogy. So, ummm...

"You really are an amateur. Note this point dear narrator, you must not assume that readers know it from the last work you have narrated. And on top of that, that work is a mixture of absurdity and whatever in the children's game nostalgia thing... Don't get confused. Think about this, if you were studying in fifth grade, and you progressed into sixth, then the maths teacher while teaching complex math problems, decided to skip certain parts using the excuse 'This part, you have learned in last grade, remember? Yes, it is' This is what you're doing now" Bright light replied.

Yes, you are right. Thanks almighty, I will keep that to my primary memory... Readers, in fiction, there exist certain rules. Am not talking about Grammar punctuation kind of thing. Ummm... There exists an ocean in fiction, which houses the soul of the characters. Each time they die in a story, their souls are transferred into a bottle, one soul per one bottle, and must remain inside it till a writer makes them appear inside their story. Little cringe but it is what it is...

Ok, where were we. Where are they? I got carried away, again! The bus has disappeared as well... Yes, found them walking, struggling with each step taken through the snowy ground. They are shivering and soon be dead for sure! Wait, what is that noise? The tour group heard it, start their search, me too... Nop, can't find anyone, must be the wind. Why are they staring at the ground? Are they all frozen to death? (gasps) No, they're not. Looks like there is someone inside this piece of snow ground, alive! The students start digging on the spot with their bare hands and all the leftover energy inside of them. They might have thought this someone is grasping for breath and was drowned inside the snow accidentally.

They finally dug him out, yes, he is he, covered in beard full of snow crystals. He is wearing shorts, nothing else. He looks alright, and he has the calmest expression I have ever seen. His yellow eyes are mesmerizing to look at, spreads a divine aura around the wretched place. He offers no appreciation to the students for digging him out. Instead orders them to follow him. As expected, the parents start questioning his motives, they raised assumptions such as:

he is an organ harvester trying to lure them into his secret lab, he is a teen molester trying to lure the kids into his den, he is a monster trying to lure them into his cave to make them his food for a month!

The mysterious man offered a smile followed by an uttered response of "Calm". The way he said it, without a slight grain of anger. How did he do that? I am sure this person is going to be the star of this difficult book. I am relieved, and am excited to learn from this man...

THREE
WELCOME

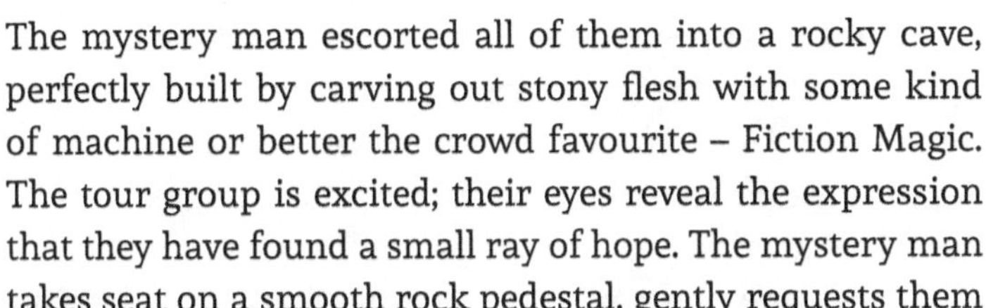

The mystery man escorted all of them into a rocky cave, perfectly built by carving out stony flesh with some kind of machine or better the crowd favourite – Fiction Magic. The tour group is excited; their eyes reveal the expression that they have found a small ray of hope. The mystery man takes seat on a smooth rock pedestal, gently requests them to take a seat on the rocky ground. The tour group accepts his request.

(splash) What the! Someone just threw a snowball right on the man's face! Come on kids, have you all lost your mind? And why the hell are these parents laughing? Am getting furious, wrath is no joke. Surprisingly, the mystery man is not affected by the uncanny behaviour, he casually wipes off the snow, keeps observing his new guests calmly with a sweet smile.

Parent: 'Stop staring at the girls, you pervert little man!'

Male Teacher: 'Sir, please help us get out of this snowy land, and am feeling hungry, some food?'

The mystery man ends his mystery, introduces himself as 'One'

One: 'Sorry to disappoint, no one can escape this place. You must stay here'

Parent: 'Yes, he is a rapist, molester like I predicted. I will break you in half if you move a muscle!'

Student: 'Stop insulting him, old man. He is alone, and even if he has any bad motive, nothing can stop him because he probably has some kind of secret weapon in his secret arsenal. But I believe he is telling the truth, his eyes emit divine rays'

Teacher: 'Sir, we must return, please help. Lot of students are dead, we must report this, and we can't stay here forever because it's like death'

One: 'I don't possess magic, understand this, there is no other way. Live here and learn'

Teacher: 'Learn what? How long can you sit here idle? And you do possess supernatural powers, if not, how could you meditate under the snowy ground, covered in snow?'

One did not answer it; he starts meditating or sleeping. I can't tell. But what I can tell is that how was he able to stay alive under the snow ground. The answer is simple, the heat emitted from human body gets trapped inside the snowy chamber, and this heat is enough to make the space warmer. I am surprised why the teacher didn't know it "Stop speaking nonsense! Human skin cannot withstand the freezing temperature of snow, but they could survive by creating a small cave with rocks, and even snow rather than directly submerging inside a pile of snow!" (someone whispered)

One: 'You can learn about the Era of Truth that will be taking birth after twenty plus years'

Teacher: 'What is that? The Era of Truth? Some kind of new theory? Recipe? Magic trick?'

One: 'It is the precious era of humanity, Good will thrive over Bad, the word "Justice" will find its rightful meaning, all sins will be engraved, peace and prosperity will reign, even the most wretched place will blossom'

Parent: 'Stop blabbering, you circus clown. Get us out of here or be prepared to die. We are all getting hungrier than ever!'

Student: 'If such a cannibalistic chaos takes action here, sure we won't be taking One first'

Student: 'What is the need of we learning about the Truth Era? We are survivors of a group that was already exhausted from years of learning, tried to find some relaxation but all spoiled. Please leave us alone'

One: 'You should learn it; there is no way to escape this place. And I am assigned by the soul of universe to guide all the refugees arriving here, into the Era of Truth'

Before anyone can make a reply to One's statement, a group of kids, male and female, made their entrance into the main spot. The parents are shocked, start calling One 'the child molester'. The twenty plus kids are wearing white robes, have the same expression of One, calm.

Kid: 'Please stop accusing our master'

Parent: 'Oh my God, what is this Devil man doing with these kids! Exploiting their innocence, turning them into slaves. Don't worry children, you won't be harmed anymore'

One: 'Please calm down. No one is exploiting anyone, and sure no one is harmed'

Teacher: 'That is not sobmething you can decide. Let the police decide, and shall give you the proper punishment'

One: 'Agreed. I hope they will find their way here somehow'

Parent: 'They will come here to rescue us shortly; your secret life is over mister master'

One: 'How about we play a game of wisdom in the meantime?'

Student: 'Let's play Guess the song'

One: 'No, my children have limited knowledge, learned from me. I received them when they were only two years old. I don't know who gave them to me, nor know how I ended up in here... If you people win the game of wisdom, I will use my secret power to get all of you back to your home'

Parents: 'Explain the game'

One: 'The Game of wisdom is played with words. My team consists of me and my children. And we will play against you. In each round, we will discuss about different aspects of human life, the team that fails to continue the discussion, or fails to answer the questions, gets defeated in that round. And your team only need to defeat us in one round to earn the victory title'

Parents: 'Let's play, shall we?'

Student: 'So, this will be The Moderns versus Ancients?'

One: 'No, it will be The Era of False versus The Era of Truth. Since you people are our guests, please start the match'

FOUR

Sacred Debate: Part One

(silence)

Teacher: 'Looks like we don't know how to play this. Please start the game, master'

One: 'Ok. My children will start the game'

Kid: 'Let's start with PEACE'

Student: 'Peace what? Are we supposed to sit quiet and meditate or something'

One: 'No, you are supposed to explain about PEACE in a sentence or a paragraph. If your team fail to answer, we will win this round, and the game will go on'

Teacher: 'Peace is what we attain after leading a successful life'

Kid: 'Explain Success'

Teacher: 'Success is... To be called worthy of being an individual by other people'

Kid: 'Explain Worthy'

Teacher: 'What is this? This is not fair, I have given the answer, let's move on. We win?'

One: 'Your answer has a lot of gaps to fill, must clarify the statement fully'

Teacher: 'Fine! Worthy is the state of being an individual earned by themselves, for their good deeds that pave way for the betterment of the society and country'

Kid: 'Explain Good Behaviour'

Teacher: 'Son of a ***** Stop playing with me ok, can somebody please help me?'

Parent: 'Calm down mister, take a seat, I know what to do... Good behaviour is... Key to... Marry... Winner...'

Student: 'Enough of your explanation, grandpa. Good behaviour is a feeling that makes other people to like you, because they feel safe around you. And you will be kind and helpful to all'

One: 'Ok, my children, it is your turn to answer. Start'

Kid: 'PEACE is the greatest gift for humanity, but only a few achieve it'

Student: 'Why not? We have experienced Peace during our... How to achieve it, you say?'

Kid: 'Having great knowledge of oneself is the key element to achieve Peace because, knowing the strength and weakness of oneself shall pave way to the elimination of jealousy, guilt and envy'

Teacher: 'How come? Explain'

One: 'We feel Jealousy, Guilt, Envy only when we compare ourselves with other people, who have used their strengths more to cover their weaknesses'

Student: 'We all have weaknesses? What is wrong with you?'

One: 'We do possess weakness; it varies from person to person. No one is perfect, heard it?'

Student: 'Yes, sir. What if I say my weakness is I can't study? am I allowed to not study at all ever again?'

One: 'If studying is your weakness, then you should try to embrace the strength you believe you have in you'

Student: 'I can't think of any strength of mine! Eating, scrolling, nothing'

One: 'Then you should study as hard as you can, you will definitely find your strength once you challenge your lazy mind by studying, reading, listening, and whatever the activities that you find challenging and not excited for'

Kid: 'For PEACE, a person must erase their negative side, this will only be possible by respecting oneself and others'

Student: 'Modern civilization is filled with buildings, tension. There is no Peace for anyone. Most people seldom get few hours of rest; sure, most people can't spend time to grind for Peace by taking journeys and other fun activities. And today's busy schedule has made true friendships extinct'

Kid: 'Locations don't matter, Heart is the ultimate location to seek Peace, if your heart doesn't have it, there is no other way than to refresh your heart from all its negative shades. Not easy'

Parent: 'How to prepare the Heart?'

Kid: 'Respect self, stay away from pride. And cheer for other people's victories, strengths. Remember the fact, human life is not a competition'

Teacher: 'Why is PEACE considered the greatest gift? mentioned by your team early, remember?'

One: 'Yes, Peace is the greatest gift, because no matter how much wealth, knowledge, pride we gain. Peace can only be gained from our own heart; it is a pure state of mind'

(silence)

One: 'We won the last round. Let's go to the next round, it's your turn, hope you remember how we played last round'

Teacher: 'How did we lose last round, pray tell?'

One: 'If a team fails to ask questions or provide answers – the team will lose the round, remember the rule?'

Teacher: 'Ok. Let's play next round. Students, take them down!'

Student: 'Ok, my question is, what is Lust? Is that something we received from our ancestors?'

Kid: 'Lust is a reminder to every species on Earth to not let their kind to go extinct, the ecosystem cycle demands it. Yes, our ancestry code does have it'

Parent: 'How to save students from getting not addicted to porn? Get them back to the study track?'

One: 'According to the Brain, the ultimate aim of existence is to multiply and enjoy. For this sole purpose, it sends massive currents of energy into every species' soul to complete the aim. And when it comes to the students, they can disturb this massive current of energy by not opting to go along with it by actively controlling it constantly, and thus creating tension inside the brain, which then turns into surplus of energy. This surplus of energy can then be transferred into other activities, and should be'

Kid: 'Who are the weakest to control it?'

(silence)

One: 'Answer it, Era of False. Forgot how this game works?'

Teacher: 'No, we were thinking. The weakest to control that urge shall be the ones who are lazy. They have already given complete freedom to their brain for making its sole dream come true. Am I right?'

One: 'Yes, that is right. Good'

Teacher: 'We won?'

One: 'Not yet, you must make us silent with a question of your own, or just explaining every aspect of the subject and thus making it impossible to form a new question for your team'

Teacher: 'Ok, how can we stop... Why is it... When can a person... Am out of questions, can somebody help me? Students, think of something... Expand the proverb, a lazy mind is a devil's workshop!'

Kid: 'Like master already explained, a lazy mind will take control of the person, making them unrest and orders this person to satisfy their sole aim according to the brain, to copulate'

One: 'Instead of being lazy, try to utilise the surplus energy to embrace their own talents. If they can't find their talent, try to force themselves on a random skill and learn it. Ok, since your team has come up with a repetitive question, your team has lost the second round'

Teacher: 'Fair defeat, we take it. Let's go for round three, we are getting used to the rules. Takes time'

(silence)

One: 'It's our turn, and let's discuss "Love", shall we?'

Student: 'Love and Lust are different entities?'

Kid: 'Yes, they are. Love is pure, while Lust is not pure. Love leads to affection, respect, caring. Meanwhile Lust's sole focus is to send urges to make everyone copulate'

One: (to a parent) 'Would you love someone if there was no possibility to have sex with this someone?'

Parent: 'Stop asking inappropriate questions you sick old man. They are college students, and you have a bunch of kids sitting next to you taking notes, and this is what you have to deliver?'

Student: 'Stop over-reacting man, I saw you checking out our teacher, stop acting like a gentleman'

Teacher: 'Everyone please calm down... Think about the question, can anyone answer it?'

Student: 'I know. If there was no possibility for sex, they can't have children?'

One: 'That's not what I asked. Forget this baby thing, focus on the emotion, Love'

Teacher: 'No, physical union of bodies is necessary for Love. There is no other way, is there?'

Student: 'Pure love doesn't exist? What is this world!'

One: 'Don't worry child, pure love does exist. It rises out from respect and admiration, not from a person's physical appearance but the qualities that person has. This respect for one's qualities should be the bond that holds relationships'

Teacher: 'Stop bragging about, what qualities are you talking about?'

Kid: 'Our master was talking about admiring a person's intellect, their talents and skills, the way this person speaks, smile, treats other people, interests and hobbies, pretty much everything this person does. The fact of the matter is, never judge a person by their physical appearance'

One: 'Different people find others attractive, based solely on their unique qualities'

Student: 'There is a survey that points out, friends fall in love with each other often. Is this true?'

One: 'Yes, my previous answer speaks for this question. Becoming good friends means that two people getting to know each other very well, and it helps them form a special bond with each other, though sometimes friendship does fail because one of them prefers to judge the other by that person's physical appearance, invoking the lustful energy'

Teacher: 'Can Lust transform into Love?'

Kid: 'Yes, there is a possibility. If two people get attracted to each other, at first, by the bond of Lust, there is a possibility for that Lust bond turning into a Love bond later, because Lust paved way for them to get to know each other the first time'

One: 'Lust acted as a wingman there, as per modern style'

Teacher: 'Love at first sight, is that real?'

One: 'Are you trying to buy more time to think of a good question or an explanation?'

Teacher: 'Yes I am. Third round lost!'

One: 'Never give up hope. There are plenty more to go, we must take a break, night is approaching, must get food'

Teacher: 'From where? What kind of deadly garbage grows in this cold wretched place?'

Kid: 'We are not going to harvest anything, just move a little, dig in the snow, get lucky. That's it for the food hunt'

Teacher: 'We will die from frostbite, please let us stay here and rest. You people are experienced in this, go and fetch something for us. When you take us to our home, we will pay you greatly. Deal?'

One: 'Don't worry, here, wear this clothing and you will be alright, it's just that we can't find food for all of you if we were to work with a small number'

Master gives suits made of tree shavings to the teachers and some of the students who are happy to help with the food hunt. Master, five Truth Era kids, both teachers, seven students marched out of the rocky cave, followed Master who is not wearing any gear and is walking ahead with no form of trouble... Finally, Master made his stop, a wide snowy land, no sign of life. Teachers and students are disappointed, and angry. Master and his Kids started digging the snowy ground with a wooden stick, meanwhile the students keep laughing at them.

I don't understand what is making them laugh like that, can't they think even the slightest? Master and his kids are living in this unfriendly place for years; sure, they know how to find food here or else they would have been dead and engraved inside this snowy cemetery place.

The laughter has stopped suddenly; Master has yanked up a transparent plastic bag full of fried rice and some kind of gravy mixed inside. Like a chain reaction, Master's kids pulled out a variety of fruits and cooked food wrapped in plastic, out of the snow. And what is more shocking is that one of the Kids pulled out a big birthday cake out of the deadly snow! The land of fiction is quite mesmerizing indeed.

The food hunt crew made their way back to the carved rocky mountain, ate plentiful, called it a day and everyone dropped to sleep, even though the bumpy rock ground is not friendly to human flesh. For the first time in this book, I have entered the fiction famous existential dilemma! As a narrator, I don't know what to do... Whoa! I can become visible now, am sure as hell this wasn't possible during the daytime, during the game rounds. Ok, I have to be careful now, I must not wake any of them. I walked slowly through the narrow line of path in between the new and old residents. "Hey you, come here" Someone called me from behind. I turned around, Master One, He is awake.

One: 'You are the narrator, aren't you?'

Me: 'Yes Master, I am him. I have become a huge fan of you. You possess sgreat amount of wisdom. Do you really believe you can transform these people?'

One: 'Yes. I do. Not the middle-aged gang but the students'

Me: 'Why not?'

One: 'There is no way to change the middle aged, they have already acknowledged that their destiny is completed, thus, they will never even try to test their long-held beliefs and ideologies, even when they are a hundred percent sure they are wrong'

Me: 'You keep amazing me, Master One'

One: 'I don't want to amaze anyone, am just passing my knowledge to others'

Me: 'With all due respect, who taught you all this? Who is that great teacher of yours. Is that who I think it is... The Soul of Fiction?'

One: 'Yes, it is. Let me tell you how I came here. Ended up here, to be clear. It all happened one day, I woke up inside this polished rocky cave, I still can't remember my life before that event. The moment I woke up inside this cave, I was like a new man, with no past. After that initial shock, I found different types of fruits scattered across this cave, along with a pile of books, fictional. Without anything to do, I put myself into the pile of books, learned all that knowledge, has become the One'

Me: 'What's with the name, One? Where did you get that?'

One: 'I got it from one of the books, because the inscription on it clearly stated that "The person who reads this book shall be the first One to enter the Era of Truth" and I took that to my heart"

Me: 'What happened to the books?'

One: 'They all disappeared after I read them full, still don't know what kind of magic that was?'

Me: 'I have to ask; how did you find out that there was food under the snowy ground. Do you cultivate? If yes, it should be violating the entire agricultural realm'

One: 'I found another inscription inside a book, "Do not worry about food, the vast snowy ground around you, is filled with plenty amount of food"

Me: 'That's cool. Guess am done with my boring questions. Do you sleep?'

One: 'Yes, Of course. But if you want company, I can stay awake. I know that you have entered the existential dilemma, I can read it on your face'

Me: 'Please don't sleep, and if you're interested, I want to hear some of the fictional contents you have read in those wisdom full books'

(silence)

FIVE

MYTHIC TALE: PART ONE

One: 'Ok. Once upon a time, there was a kingdom called "Bigrench" and was ruled by angry cannibals. The normal human beings suffered under the brutal rules established by the cannibal leaders. Due to their mighty profile, no one dared to challenge their cruel authority. Their brutish rules were mandatory self-sacrifice every week, women who were not pregnant or not rearing a child were obliged to visit the mansion every week, no form of grouping up was allowed etc. The people were all looking skinny as a stick, skeletons put inside a dress made of skin. They all looked uniform with their red robe dress. The brutish mercenaries identified women by remembering two things: long hair, no facial hair.

People there could not recollect their past life before arriving Bigrench, but they were sure they were not born here. Bigrench kingdom was indeed a wretched place, devoid of vegetation because of the steaming ground it had. People tried digging the ground but flaming liquid kept sprouting out of the holes. The inhabitants were not supplied anything by the authority either, they remained starving but not met with death. Bigrench had no boundaries but had one mysterious door that looked like it was freestanding on the ground, new people were pushed out of that door when it opened for a split second. And it was through that door, the mighty Cadevar arrived there.

Cadevar was special compared to the others, he was huge in size, but nothing compared to the cannibal leaders ruling the place. Cadevar was given a warm welcome by the inhabitants, and they immediately begged him to sacrifice himself to become food for them. Cadevar was shocked.

Cadevar: 'Why? What is this place? Are we supposed to feast on each other? What is that castle?'

Someone: 'We are starving for years, can't tolerate the pain, if you please accept our request, we can all experience what it is like to be not starving'

Someone: 'That castle belongs to the authority, they randomly pick us to satisfy their hunger'

Cadevar: 'Me accepting your request can only offer temporary satisfaction, what about fighting them? I can lead you'

Someone: 'Look at us, we can barely walk, we don't know if we at least have a gram of flesh for the hungry beasts to take'

The crowd dispersed. Cadevar joined the community, though he didn't give them what they wanted, they showed no anger to him. Cadevar, along with the others started following the routines, which was nothing but to walk around the walls surrounding the castle of cannibals. They did this walk to feel the cold breeze that was oozed out of the walls, and for this same reason, all of them were hoping to get picked by the leaders for whatever madness they wanted them for. Sleeping was not possible, the flaming hot ground was not friendly to human skin, the sound of nonstop sizzling filled the air all the time due to the inescapable foot burn.

Cadevar was a careful observer, he had one thing in his mind all the time, to defeat the cannibals and take the kingdom. He forged a plan and the community agreed to it, the plan was that he would dress like a woman and enter the castle. The community agreed without second thought because they had faith in Cadevar, and it was not the first time someone mentioned this plan. Before Cadevar asked for anything, a woman ripped off her hair and gave it to him, and with a heated rock, Cadevar shaved his face clean. The woman who gave her hair to Cadevar, approached him and made him promise not to drop her hair.

Cadevar was surprised by her promise thing. He planned to reveal his identity the moment he enters the castle, and then to engage in melee combat. The mercenaries came to take the women; their first pick was Cadevar. They escorted him and six women into the castle, Cadevar suppressed his nerves to keep the promise alive. He was thunder-stricken by the amount of beauty the castle had. The guards took the six women into a prison cell but forced Cadevar into a royal room decorated lavishly. He was made to sit on a massive bed and was left alone. Cadevar took his opportunity and wandered around the castle.

Even though some of the guards saw him, none of them cared to take him seriously. He found a large room filled with cooked meat, stacked like a haystack and he had the courage to take a bite out of it. Cadevar then found the infamous prison cell, made of bricks, which was locked but could see through the narrow gaps. He found skinny to normal women inside of it, he then went back to bed he was first made to sit. Cadevar kept waiting for many hours, he lost his patience, ran around. The castle was emptied. There was no one, they all disappeared from the place. Cadevar released the locked-up women and other prisoners inside the dungeon underground.

Cadevar opened the main gate, the skinny population joyfully entered the castle. They immediately went inside the room filled with stacks of cooked meat, the long years of starvation improved their olfactory senses beyond any other being. They emptied the whole meat stacks! Praised Cadevar and made him their King. Cadevar was in disbelief, but he decided to take the King post. The castle was standing in the middle of a vast area of land, and unlike the wretched ground outside the castle wall, the vast ground surrounding the building was perfect for cultivation. Cadevar's subjects started farming there and received unbelievable yield in a day.

Cadevar had little to worry about his duty as the King because his subjects were the innocent human beings ever lived. After a week, Cadevar's people transformed massively. Their previous 'dress on a stick' appearance was no more. Cadevar divided the community into farmers and warriors, took extra care in forming an army, because he was sure about an attack happening anytime. After a month, the whole community became unrest, violence against women increased. Cadevar introduced the marriage paradigm to satisfy his subjects' carnal hungers, and it succeeded.

The introduction of marriage paved way for families and newborn. Happiness spread across the castle. But after a few years, the sexual unrest returned. This time it was the newly arrived bachelor men, who never had the chance to marry because of the small number of woman population the Kingdom had. Cadevar advised them to control themselves and focus more on battle training. Married men population received a serious hit with a chain of murders. Cadevar knew what the reason was, and he decided to introduce the infamous brothel, filled them with widows.

Things were under control for almost a year but then came the ultimate issue. The whole place filled with abandoned babies. What happened was that, after the introduction of brothels for the newly arrived, the loyal people who were married, betrayed their loyalty and fulfilled their dirty wishes inside the brothel. This led to the horrible situation where every single newborn was thrown away into the bushes. The entire castle turned into a brothel, and Cadevar was thrown out of it for his disapproval of the current scenario. And finally, the cannibal leaders returned out of nowhere, they used their brutal methods to regain their castle back.

In a few minutes, the brothel loving community joined Cadevar outside the castle walls. After a month, they were all transformed back to their old skinny profile, Cadevar also turned into the skinniest version of him. They all restarted their daily routine of walking around the castle walls' (One's narration ends)

Me: 'And then came the next Cadevar, loop story?'

One: 'You decide, did you get the moral of the story?'

Me: 'They all wrapped in Sins after getting comfortable with their lives, they brought the doom upon themselves'

One: 'What should they have done?'

Me: 'They should have prepared for any upcoming attack, must have formed an army, built an alliance, formed strategies, fortified the place'

One: 'But they did nothing but filled themselves with pleasure. Forgot all the struggles they suffered for a long number of years'

Me: 'They took their new fortune for granted'

One: 'Exactly. Instead of trying to figure out what happened to their cruel leaders and preparing for the future, they welcomed the Sins into themselves'

Me: 'It is like when people don't value something till it's gone. I do remember that when I was narrating the previous work, I was angry and had no satisfaction from that work. But when I was back inside the lonely bottle, I felt guilty for not enjoying my narration life. And now that I am inside another work, I do feel bored and angry. It is a constant feeling'

One: 'It is because, when you have time and space to think about yourself and other aspects of your life, you will figure out what's best and worst for you. But things will be different when you drop out of your mind, due to the intervention of outside forces, including the negative shades'

Me: 'Maybe Cadevar's subjects were exhausted from all of their sufferings, and the years of trouble made them vulnerable to the evil side of theirs'

One: 'Yes. Cadevar's subjects had two choices, either to embrace the good side or the bad side of theirs –

(footsteps)

Me: 'Who is that? I should turn invisible... Student, what is he doing at this time. Poor Master'

One: 'What is the problem, son? What makes you not asleep?'

Student: 'Master, I have become a huge fan of yours. Can you please help me make that beautiful girl to fall in love with me?'

One: 'She is one of my kids, you are so brave to ask me this. Tell me about yourself'

Student: 'Well, am caring and sweet. And I have never been in a relationship. I promise I will never cheat her'

One: 'What about your career? Have you identified your strengths? Can you promise me that you are not attracted to her physical appearance?'

Student: 'No, my love is very pure, it has nothing to do with her body, and I promise you I will never touch her before we get married'

One: 'What made you fall in love with her?'

Student: 'Love at first sight, I strongly believe she has a good heart and soul'

One: 'How come? And you still not answered my question about your strength'

Student: 'I go to the gym every day, have a great amount of strength in my body, does that count?'

One: 'Yes, it does count. Be optimistic, son. Why doubt your skills? taking care of your own health is appreciative. Only a few people do that'

Student: 'I never thought like such. My parents have no interest in me going to the gym, wasting valuable time there. They accused me of taking gym membership as an excuse to not study' (cries)

One: 'Calm down son. I understand your feelings; you are a nice person. And what other skills you have? It is perfectly alright to say "nothing else" I won't think less of you'

Student: 'I was good at drawing, have won medals back in my school days'

One: 'What happened after school? Have you stopped drawing?'

Student: 'I had to, because I was burdened with the need to concentrate on my studies'

One: 'Why didn't you study and draw? That was a mistake, you should have done both. Son, it doesn't matter whether you score high or low, the important thing is to study for the exams'

Student: 'Master, hear me please. It was my parents who forced me to quit drawing, to not waste time. I was innocent'

One: 'Sorry dear, it was still your fault. If you love to do something, then you should pick a fight with anyone to defend yourself. And don't worry, your time is not over. You can start drawing from now on, my blessings. And don't forget to visit the Gym, keep that in mind'

Student: 'I really doubt myself. I am not confident enough to follow my heart'

One: 'Show me your palm... You see this line, it is the line of creative genius, and these branched lines are bundle of beauty with soul. Let me take a look in your eyes, please open them wide... Yes, my doubts are confirmed, you will become an artistic painter and will earn enough money to lead a satisfactory life. Happy now?'

Student: 'Thank you Master'

(silence)

Me: 'Whoa! What just happened? He has completely forgot about why he met you. What kind of magic was that?'

One: 'It was no magic. When he first approached me, he had low self-esteem, confidence and a heavy load of insecurities. The reason he chose to make one of my Kids his romantic partner, was his plan to cover all his insecurities'

Me: 'How can someone does that? Does that work?'

One: 'Yes, it does work. You see; by entering a relationship, he will get the feeling that he is worthy to be loved'

Me: 'Why he feels like that? Is that really an achievement?'

One: 'In the animal kingdom, yes. Do you have any knowledge of the history of living beings? The animal kingdom has three objectives to complete, to find/hunt food, to fight intruders and most importantly to secure a mate to copulate. I was talking about this final objective. Get it?'

Me': 'Yes, I get it. But are you sure that going to the gym is a skill? No, I mean, is that something that needs appreciation'

One: 'Why not? It is indeed a skill and needs to be appreciated, because it will build respect to oneself and it is a good way to drain out the surplus of energy that I have mentioned before'

Me: 'Anyway, morning has arrived. Guess I should become invisible and start narrating the rest of the competition you have here. Bye master'

One: 'Have fun narrating'

Teacher: 'Whom are you talking to? Shall we start the next round?'

One: 'Why so hurry? Let the others come to life as well, be patient, son'

Teacher: 'Hey everyone, get up! The match is about to start; don't you all need to go home?'

Student: 'Yes sir, let's go. Who will start? Anyone prepared?'

SIX

SACRED DEBATE: PART TWO

Teacher: 'I am. What is Life? Is it worth to live?'

One: 'It's a personal choice, but yes, it is'

Teacher: 'Is life meaningful? Explain'

One: 'Life should be meaningful, and if you think that it is not meaningful, then you should give it away by engaging in selfless acts, by helping others in need'

Parents: 'That is what we call "working" except we all get paid'

Student: 'What if a person decides to end their own life because they have found it meaningless and not worth?'

Kid: 'To commit suicide is the most sinful action a person can do. Because it is a statement that the person has no respect for Earth'

Student: 'Earth? Really? There are over eight billion plus human beings that Earth must worry about'

One: 'Respect for Earth means that, the respect a person should have for all the essential elements provided by the Earth, in the form of water, food, air etc. Opting to end life by oneself is a sin'

Teacher: 'How to make Life more meaningful?'

Student: 'Does it require super high scores, conquering the mountains, getting a good, reputed job, getting married before Thirty!'

Parent: 'Yes, so you do know. Why still fail?'

Kid: 'To make life meaningful, try to give your time, wealth, love, kindness to those in need. They will do that to others as well as to you. This cycle of 'give and receive' built with respect and care is enough to make life meaningful'

Parent: 'Stop playing with meanings. What is Life? Provide a definition, will you?'

One: 'Life is an opportunity to better us by working for ourselves, using our unique talents and dedication, helping other people to better themselves, celebrating each other's victories and achievements, paving way for new participants-

Teacher: 'It is a competition indeed, right?'

One: 'Yes, a competition to spread happiness and help others, because when you help people in need, they will pass the favour and help other people in need, at least the person who helped them once'

Parent: 'What a boring explanation that was! You are literally advising everyone to giveaway their hard-earned money and carelessly wait for someone to return the money to repeat the cycle. It is not surprising that how you came up with such weird explanations, a man who is spending his entire life inside a weird cave hole, with a group of innocent children- who gave you permission to corrupt these little kids!'

One: 'I was not talking about money alone. Money is not the only thing people need help with. They crave for care, support, opinions, even someone to share their thoughts to, will be more than enough for most people. Money is just a part inside this helping cycle. Everyone deserves the opportunity to enjoy life, and it is up to everyone to check on others, at least people they are closer to, to see how they are doing'

Parent: 'If everyone works hard, they can become happy without others help. What about that?'

Kid: 'Define Happy. When was the last time you experienced happiness? What are the things that make you happy?'

Parent: 'That's a lot of questions, from a Kid! Anyway, Happiness is the feeling that wraps you whole when you do things that are proven to bring you happiness'

One: 'What are those things?'

Parent: 'Hmmm... Like going on a vacation, watching a movie, travelling... Exploring'

One: 'When was the last time you did one of these proven methods, and which one?'

Parent: 'Travelling, me and my family went for a trip to the Meblon Garden Valley last month. I was very happy during that trip'

One: 'Happy for what? Tell me about the interesting things you have witnessed in that journey'

Parent: 'Hmmm... The photos, my kids smile... the food...'

One: 'So, you didn't feel happiness inside you just by watching the scenes happening all around you?'

Parent: 'No'

Kid: 'Why is that? Is that a universal thing?'

Teacher: 'Yes, my dear, it is universal. The moment a man decides to become a father, his happiness will be sucked out of him, and then placed on to his child'

One: 'What a weird way of explanation that was? Anyway, mister Parent, you do agree that you became happy seeing your child's happy smile. Do you still remember what were we talking about before we got carried away too much? The answer is Life and helping others happy. What is making you take a step back from making a random person happy?'

Parent: 'I don't know. I have never received such care from any stranger, not even from my close relatives either. Then why would I think about helping others! It's not fair'

One: 'Someone has to start it, don't you think?'

Parent: 'Totally agree but am already past that time. Let the youngsters take care of that'

One: 'I hope so'

Teacher: 'What about the people who elaborate on the subject, life is meaningless? I strongly believe they have some point'

One: 'There are two types of people who would say that, first we have the lazy people who use this theory as an excuse to take life for granted, they boast about what is the purpose for all that hard work, sleep is the ultimate reward for them. Then there is the second group of people who are similar to the Parent we talked to minutes before, they have never received the pleasure of experiencing any selfless act from someone, no one cared to offer them help let alone have a talk with them. And because of this, the second group has used the thought of meaningless Life to explain what made their lives miserable. They have their reasons, but it is not right to call Life meaningless, because this thought will summon up a lot of negative ways to live Life'

(silence)

Teacher: 'Ok, Master. Your team won that round. I must say that you are indeed a man of wisdom'

One: 'Shall we go to the next round?'

Teacher: 'Sure. Kids, your turn'

Kid: 'MERCY. Why is it so important?'

Teacher: 'Humans are prone to make errors, aren't they?'

Student: 'Sir, please answer with not a question. Sorry master, let me take that one. Mercy is important, because it is the only thing we need to lead a perfect life'

Parent: 'Oh, really? What would you do when someone pours hot coffee all over you? Or what if someone makes a sudden stop in the middle of a highway when you're driving?'

Student: 'Ummm... I am not really the mercy type, please somebody help me'

Teacher: 'We learn from our mistakes, and if someone is physically or mentally hurt by that mistake of ours, that someone should have mercy'

Student: 'Why are you keep answering in an interrogative tone? Please complete your sentences, dang it!'

Parent: 'What did you say last?'

Student: 'I take that back. Sorry sir'

Teacher: 'Yeah whatever. Did we lose that one too? Great!'

One: 'Please continue. Stop using textbook type explanations. Just remember the last time you forgave someone'

Teacher: 'Does forgiving your students for not completing the homework count?'

Student: 'Stop being silly! Sorry master, I will answer... Last month, when I was standing at the bus stop, watching social media, out of nowhere: someone ran past me and he accidentally or not stepped on my foot, didn't care to offer me an apology. I am not angry'

Parent: 'I have something to say, last year, when I was taking a stroll down the street, dressed in perfect condition to attend a bachelor party, suddenly, I was covered in filth.

The people living on top of a building did it, I saw them emptying their garbage bin when I took a quick peek at the top. I went back to my apartment, changed my dress. Not angry'

Teacher: 'Let me add something, last year when I was driving my car, someone kept honking behind my car. I couldn't let him get away because there was a vehicle stampede on the other lane. He continued pressing his irritating horn sound, and when he finally overtook me, he stopped his car and stepped out only to worship me with cuss words, even had the courage to throw a medium size stone at me, luckily it didn't hit the vulnerable parts. Not angry'

One: 'I am surprised why did all of you three repeat the phrase "Not angry", the fact that the three of you can still remember such incidents is because you three still have grudge over them'

Teacher: 'Yeah. I do. Why is that?'

One: 'All of the bad incidents you three have mentioned, the moment when they have happened, Wrath has taken birth in each of you, and each time you keep remembering the incident, this Wrath will fuel it more'

Student: 'Who is Wrath? Master, you are speaking like it is an entity. And why didn't it make us take revenge the moment they happened?'

One: 'Wrath is an entity; it co-exists with oneself. And when bad events like you have mentioned happens, Wrath takes control of the person's consciousness, making them unrest and guilty'

Parent: 'Guilty for what?'

Student: 'Why it didn't take revenge the moment the events happened?'

One: 'Guilty for making their self less-respected, devalued, and a coward in the eyes of others. Human beings love to seek other people's validation, and they think of themselves as superior to most. When someone refuses to give an apology, the victim will feel that the offender is winning against the victim's self, stealing the victim's humane progress. Human mind is very complex; science enthusiasts are still not completely able to decipher the complex working of human brain'

Student: 'Master, please answer my question'

One: 'The Human mind is instinctually programmed to defeat other humans, and to become first by using whatever brutal means necessary. But due to their intellectual qualities and their unique quality to find out the depths of the undiscovered and the forbidden things, humans have made advancements in every form of knowledge, this created an artificial cover over themselves to cover their selfish instinctual flaws. And when it comes to the bad events we have discussed earlier, the artificial cover made them not react immediately, the withstanding capacity of this cover varies from person to person, some people have no cover at all, causing the instant raged up Wrath to explode in its full essence. Now, the Wrath-suppressers keep boiling their unfulfilled explosion, enough to create extreme destruction. Wrath tries hard to provoke the host to do its bidding, some may fall for it while the strongest fight and conquer it'

Student: 'How to conquer it? Enlighten us Master'

Parent: 'Study more, get a job, start a family'

Teacher: 'Sir, can you please stay silent! Let the Master speak'

One: 'Conquering Wrath is harder than anything. The whole punishment book was created to imprison Wrath.

But people still engage in brutality. The only way to succumb it is to let the Wrathful get away'

Student: 'What do you mean by that? Let the person hurt anyone they want? How is that going to work?'

One: 'As long as the Wrathful person's deeds are not crossing the limit, the Merciful must counter the Wrathful by not engaging in combat of any form'

Teacher: 'But the Wrathful will take the victory over the merciful, that is not fair. The good always win, right?'

One: 'Let me explain a scenario, a good man and an evil man are fighting, and the only way to stop the evil man is by killing him. The good man finally does it, he has killed the bad man but at the same time he himself became an evil man'

Teacher: 'Yes Master, please continue...'

One: 'Mercy is infectious, it will spread in high volume and rapidly. The person countering Wrath will be able to replace the devil with the angel, i.e. Mercy'

Teacher: 'Is Mercy something that we have in ourselves, but concealed in some way?'

One: 'I will answer that question in the last round, trust me'

Student: 'Why is Mercy infections? And what if the Wrathful takes advantage of the Merciful?'

One: 'You are talking about things like Greed, Envy. Wrath is not concerned about anything but rage. It has no concerns for the consequences of an action or a thought. Wrath needs pleasure from participation in ravenous activities forbidden by the law. And Mercy is infectious; think about the last time someone has given you Mercy'

Student: 'Oh, that's a tough one... Found one, two years ago, when I was riding my bicycle, I rode down a steep narrow road. Mid-way, I saw a middle-aged man walking through the middle of the road. I pressed the bell, the man heard it and he moved a step to the right without looking back. I steered to the left side without second thought, but he changed his mind in a fraction of a second, took three steps to the left. I tried my best to stop the ride, but the front tyre made its bold landing mark over the calves of that man. Surprisingly, he smiled and forgave me'

One: 'That's a heart-warming experience. You did physical damage to that person and he remained calm. And now, what would you do if you find yourself in a situation similar to that Mercy guy incident? Will you forgive him?'

Student: 'I will forgive that person. Mercy is infectious indeed. Thank you, Master'

One: 'And if the person didn't give you forgiveness, instead cussed you all over, you would have done the same to your offender'

(silence)

One: 'I believe it's your team's turn'

Student: 'I will start this time... Marriage!'

One: 'It is one's personal choice'

Parent: 'What! Sir, please don't put negative shade over the most beautiful thing a human being can take part in their whole lifetime'

Student: 'It is the weirdest ceremony ever!'

One: 'Why son? What made you say so?'

Student: 'I don't like this marriage agreement. To make future generation! What is that?'

Parent: 'No future? Is that what you want, huh? I see, you're one of those friends with benefits living together type, aren't you? Abortion rates are increasing every year because of all that nonsense, not to mention the millions of poor babies getting dumped into the street every year because of your kind of teen fathers who don't have the means to provide child support!'

Student: 'Please don't try to slide this away into other issues. Discuss the agreement called marriage, and what is the need of it being forced into most people's lives?'

Teacher: 'No one is getting forced to do anything. And believe it or not, it is because of marriage, the so-called social contract, many relationships are still stable and loyal'

Student: 'Sir, please don't agree to such nonsense. You're an educated person. Just... Master please provide a good answer'

One: 'Please... Everybody just calm down. The word Marriage cannot be explained in a sentence or two. First, we have to understand the whole root cause behind it. How it came into existence? Can anyone reflect on that?'

Teacher: 'Ummm... Marriage is essential to get a companion for life. Human beings need someone to take care of them, love them and enjoy the world with them, especially one trusted and loyal companion, bound with the laws of marriage'

One: 'Parents, anything to add?'

Parent: 'Life will be meaningless without marriage. Marry, live together, raise a baby, let them carry their parents name forward. The whole cycle thing'

One: 'Ok. Students? Your thoughts on the root cause?'

Student: 'The Sad people found a way to restrict other people who were enjoying their lives with parties, going journeys, love'

One: 'Ok. Student, what are the most common problems of this whole Marriage thing?'

Student: 'Marriage is a trap, people get matched mostly based on less compatibility, most are forced. Marriage has less success rate, brutal killings because of cheatings are filling the headlines. It is boring'

One: 'Ok. My kids, you have listened to all of this, provide the answers for them'

Kid: 'Yes Master. Men are predators, Women are preys. Marriage was invented to not let the predators' prey on every prey they can find, because that would result in a chaotic ecosystem, and might lead to the problem of some of the weak predators getting rejected from the hunt, due to their less body strength'

Parent: 'What was that? Why did you address Men as predators? sounds very aggressive'

One: 'Bravo my child. Wonderful explanation. And you mister Parent, I believe you have a daughter, and don't you worry about her, if she were to go out with some of her male friends? Why worry?'

Parent: 'How can I be not worried! People will judge her as bad, and mostly I am concerned about her male friends attacking her. That's why marriages are invented, she can enjoy her life with the chosen one'

One: 'The whole problem with marriage is due to the fact that Men are getting judged and valued down as predators, they are labelled as dangerous by both men and women'

Parent: 'We don't label every man dangerous, but no one can deny the fact that some men are dangerous'

One: 'Can you explain the reason why some men are dangerous and some are not?'

Teacher: 'It's obvious. Some men are raised well, while some are not. And some of them better themselves with the power of knowledge, while some spend their time dreaming weird unrealistic fantasies'

One: 'It is fifty – fifty?'

Teacher: 'Can't tell. But it is definitely something to be given specific attention, for the betterment of the world'

One: 'Ok, am done with male interpretation regarding the subject. I request any of the girl student to provide their opinion regarding the matter. You really think yourself as the prey?'

Student: 'It depends, sir, but I get irritated when someone is staring at me. When it comes to my campus life, I never felt like a prey, my male friends respect me, it helped me feel better'

Parent: 'Don't you have any female friends?'

One: 'Daughter of this parent, can you please raise your hand and provide an explanation for the previous question I have asked'

Parent: 'She is not ready to answer your spicy questions, keep my daughter's presence out of your jaundice eyes!'

Student: 'Master, don't mind my father. I actually feel myself as a prey, but I don't have any male friends. I am one of the invisible type students found in every classroom out there in the world. Don't look surprised class! I know you people never gave a thing about my presence in the classroom, but none of you had the mind to understand why I behaved like that. My father always taught me to stay away from males, didn't even let me message them. That's why I grew up with a mind that always judged myself as prey to the whole male species. Thank you master for giving me this opportunity to speak my soul out'

One: 'Thank you dear. Don't you see the problem, mister parent sir?'

Parent: 'Yes, I shouldn't have agreed to this trip!'

Student: 'Oh please. Master, please provide a precise explanation of the term, Marriage. How much worse is it?'

One: 'Marriage is not the worst. Marriage does come with benefits also. Don't laugh at me, patiently listen. Marriage can help family wealth getting shared, one poor family can be saved by a middle-class family through the bond of marriage, and think about the scenario where one less-wisdom person marries one high-wisdom person who can share their knowledge to the less-wisdom person, this will create a knowledge transfer cycle there'

Student: 'This whole thing is confusing. Master, please... Can we please not discuss about the sharing caring stuff, and focus only on the mental aspects?'

One: 'Sure dear, like I mentioned a few minutes earlier, treating men as predators and keeping them away from women is not a healthy treatment. Instead, friendship bonds between them should be praised. Teach men and women how to respect each other, and make them understand the boundaries each should be putting around them for sustaining the healthy bond'

Student: 'What boundaries? There are no boundaries in the mighty bond called Friendship'

One: 'No, the lack of understanding of personal and mental boundaries are the reason for the thought, Men are predators. Boundaries are necessary to let men and women keep themselves away from pesky illusive fantasies formed from Lust'

Parent: 'Who will teach them that?'

Teacher: 'It should be you parents, and us the teachers. We have great difficulty talking about personal and emotional topics in front of our students, we should improve ourselves'

One: 'Men and Women possess unique abilities, if they were to work in good harmony, they can make wonders. I know it takes time and dedication. I am hoping for a future in which Marriages won't be happening only for Lust satisfaction'

Student: 'Master, what about Marriage ceremony, the function? Any thought on that?'

One: 'Expensive marriage ceremonies are not good, because it is solely conducted to show pride and for publicly announcing that the newly married couple are off of the predator – prey list'

Parent: 'Why do you keep criticizing our beloved functions? You know how much happy people are, especially the bride and groom, on their wedding day? Oh right, how can you know, you are just the master of a lifeless plateau!'

Teacher: 'Don't mind him Master, but marriage ceremonies are good because of how many job opportunities it has created, helping many people earn money'

One: 'Yes, I know that. But think about the fact that even poor families are forced to spend an excess amount of money for conducting the ceremony, for the sake of announcing the changes done to the creepy list. And most of those families will then enter the brutal realm of debt'

Teacher: 'No one is forced. It is their own choice. And what about the upper-class people?'

One: 'Most of the middle – upper class people act miserly for their entire lifetime to conduct this one ceremony. They show no pity to others, am not talking about strangers, but their own bloodline. The main reason why marriage ceremonies are treated with utmost care is the fact that they symbolise the legal agreement for two people to satisfy their Lust, and the beginning of the next cycle of generation, that takes place with the baby shower ceremony, and other ceremonies finally ending with the funeral ceremony. The entire scheduled element created for human life, is built on the strong foundation of selfishness.

Anyone know why?'

Teacher: 'Families matter. What else should a person do? Are you advocating people to not copulate and turn the whole Earth into a wretched piece of Wasteland!'

One: 'I am advocating people to not do things against their will. And your question about "what else should a person do" is very wrong'

Teacher: 'Grammatically? Sorry. But meaning-wise, my question is acknowledged by the whole world. The only purpose of human beings is to get a job, marry, create better offsprings for the future'

Student: 'Why are you keep repeating the weird statements repeatedly! Master has already answered most of your weird questions, and why do you keep ignoring his wisdom full answers?'

Teacher: 'What did he say? His answers were all paradoxical! He does support marriage, and then suddenly, despise it. What's up with that?'

One: 'Ok, I know what you are referring to? Let me clarify my answers again, plus your final question. First, Marriages are not unhealthy, but forcing someone to marry a less compatible person is unhealthy. People with shared interests should marry. And for this state to happen, men and women should live in a healthy society in which the predator – prey category does not exist. Ok, I have already mentioned about what to do for the elimination of it. Now, the next problem is the pattern or the so-called schedule that a newly married couple is forced to follow. Not everyone is capable of parenting, running a family, look after others, or even getting married to another person. Taking these factors into consideration, it is clear that the creation of a universal life pattern is not possible. People opting to become parents should be given lectures on the matter, and financial support from the government'

Parent: 'Nonsense! Government has other important matters to do. And if a man is unable to provide for his child, then he should not marry at all'

Student: 'Can somebody please stuff a piece of cloth in his mouth! Sorry Master, but asking the Government for child support is a bit inconsiderate, isn't it?'

One: 'Considering the harmful effects suffering by the world population because of – over population, how children are abused due to careless parenting and by the abandoning of numerous children because of unwanted pregnancies, that lead to the increase of child labour – Government should take actions regarding the population crisis, and by offering financial support to parents, it gives the authority power to take actions against the parents if they were to not adhere to parental responsibilities'

(silence)

SEVEN

MYTHIC TALE: PART TWO

Another night has arrived, debates ceased, everyone is sleeping peacefully.

Me: 'Master, ready to narrate next story?'

One: 'Sure. Shall I begin?'

Me: 'Am so sorry master, I don't like to disturb your rest time, but I speak for the readers. And they want something fancy inside a book. No offence'

One: 'None taken. And don't worry about disturbing my rest time. I don't want to take rest, I do want to tell you this story because I know, as the main character in this book, my duty is to educate the readers. I do agree with your concerns regarding the book lacking a fictional base. Hope my little stories help'

Me: 'Thanks for understanding me, Master. Am ready to catch every word of yours. Please begin your next "once upon a time" narration'

One: 'Once upon a time, there was a place called Midtory. What was unique about this place was the geographical style of it, one big mountain with one magical door at the bottom and one at the top. People entering Midtory must live on the steep mountain, that had big hollow rocks perfect for sheltering inside of it, but the ground was fertile, and a constant stream of sparkling water flowed from the top, only made its stop at the bottom. Nothing to worry in terms of living conditions. Next to the door at the bottom, there was a huge pit pumping out heat waves constantly, and people of Midtory sometimes voluntarily jumped into it.

The top of the mountain could only be assessed individually, and each person could visit it once a year. Because, at the top, there was a small building next to the entrance to somewhere. Inside that building, a strange looking man lived, and he was assigned to conduct interviews with the people coming to the mountain top. He was strange looking, entire body covered in a variety of flowers but had the voice of a male human. The longest resident of Midtory spent only thirty years before getting their entrance to the top door, except for one individual named Binemil. He was the strongest person lived in Midtory due to his long stay there for over a thousand years.

Binemil had no friends there, knew no one. He was so frustrated with his fate, but his strong physique was a blessing for the Midtory community, because he was single handily capable of farming the hard ground. Binemil became angry whenever he failed to find old faces among the residents, but he was calmed when the newcomers offered him the respect of seniority. After a gap of five plus years, he decided to attempt his yearly test. Binemil slowly made his ascent to the top, and because of his enormous size, he was unable to get inside. The Gateman sensed Binemil's presence, stepped outside to conduct the interview.

Gateman: 'You are an abomination! I feel pity for your sad fate, jump into that pit please'

Binemil: 'Will think about that. What else?'

Gateman: 'Thief! You are the one who stole my flower wand last year. Where is that? How irritating you are!'

Binemil: 'I stole nothing. Don't accuse me... For what do you hate me? Come on, I have spent over a thousand years living here, let me go through'

Gateman: 'You stole nothing? Where is nothing now? I knew it was you. Don't you have any shame of revealing your theft of something valuable like nothing?'

Binemil became angry and stormed off, a pattern that kept following him. Binemil waited for the next year, time came. He went to the top, Gateman stepped outside,

Gateman: 'Two years in a row. Didn't take my advice! Ok. Tell me about your qualities. Remember, eating is not one'

Binemil was filled with rage, but he pretended to be cool and answered his question

Binemil: 'I am hard working, helpful, handsome'

Gateman: 'Hard working to eat alone selfishly to maintain ugliness. Mic drop!'

Binemil: 'I am not selfish; I do most of the farming duties here without any assistance from others. Am like a brazen bull'

Gateman: 'How dare you call me a Bull?'

Binemil: 'No, I meant me, am the Bull'

Gateman: 'Oh, so you just want to kill me by turning yourself into a Bull (laughs) even a real Bull will get scared seeing you'

Binemil left the mountain top. And every time he descended there, each step he took created massive shock waves throughout the ground, and it was enough to make the ground ready to be fertile again. Binemil waited patiently for his 'third year in a row' appearance at the top. Once again, the time came, he slowly went to the top. Gateman stepped out but this time he was holding on to a half-bitten apple.

Gateman: 'What!'

Binemil: 'I am ready Sire. Let me inside'

Gateman: 'Inside what? This apple? (throws the Apple to Binemil's face, it exploded on impact) Happy?'

Surprisingly, Binemil stood there staring at the Gateman.

Gateman: 'Sit on the ground!'

Binemil sat on the ground, but the Gateman then hand signalled him to get up immediately. Binemil jumped up

Gateman: 'Who told you to stand up! Why so dumb?'

That was it. Binemil made his descend. He swore himself not to meet the Gateman ever again. Binemil spent the next decade toiling hard on the hard ground, turned the massive rocks into cottages by carving them out, helped to build houses for the new residents. Binemil engaged in intense strength activities to drain his anger off. Each time when he noticed someone missing from his new friend's group, he became enraged. And one time, Binemil became angry enough to descend his way down to the bottom of the mountain, where the heat pit was. Binemil was determined to jump into it but at the last moment, someone grabbed his legs. It was a Kid.

Kid: 'Please don't, you are good. You deserve better. Come with me, and help me'

Binemil: 'Who are you kid? How did you end up here?'

Kid: 'I don't know my name, and don't know how I came here. And I need your help, please guide me here'

Binemil explained to the kid about the whole place, and how it worked. The Kid was amazed and wanted to visit the Gateman, excited for his first attempt with the infamous Gateman, the Kid climbed to the top with sheer speed. Binemil sat on a rock, waited for the Kid's return because he had made the Kid promise Binemil that he would meet Binemil no matter what happened at the top. The Kid stepped into the small building of the Gateman. Kid was stunned after seeing the wet flowers covering the walls, ground, ceiling. No windows. He roamed around there, picked a few flowers. The Gateman hiding in a corner grabbed the Kid's hand. (loud scream)

Gateman: 'Stop screaming you little human. Lost your way to the nursery? Parents forgot to come?' (laughs)

Kid: (laughs) 'Nice joke, uncle. Can I have that red flower?'

Gateman: 'No. What will you do? Cry?' (laughs and throws a half-eaten mango at the kid's feet, no reaction from kid)

Kid: 'Why are you staring at me sir? Am I supposed to smile?'

Gateman: 'No, you are supposed to be scared'

Kid: 'Didn't feel a thing. Try again or else I will pick that red flower off your middle'

Gateman: 'Kid, Kid, Kid... Binemil sent you here, didn't he? That rat dumpster, Kid you need to stay away from that man. And you can go, see you next year'

Gateman made a snap with his left hand, and it was enough to teleport the Kid back to the bottom of the mountain. Kid found a folded note sticking on his forehead, he pulled it off, it said "note from the Gateman: If you ever act smart in front of me again, next time you will be spawned on top of that heat pit. Understand! Little piece of advice, stay away from that big old man of foolishness" Kid ignored his advice, climbed all the way to the middle, met Binemil.

Kid: 'Binemil, I saw what is behind that gate!'

Binemil: 'What! You need a dramatic moment to tell? Spit it out!' (jumps up aggressively)

Kid: 'It is just another mountain, but less steep, that's it'

Binemil: 'What? Are you lying? I cursed myself for over a thousand years for that!'

Kid: 'What were your expectations?'

Binemil: 'I don't know. I thought it would be better than this place. The flower guy said I was unworthy, to my face. What's up with that?'

Kid: 'He just wanted to make you feel bad, because you are strong and powerful. Nobody can defeat you, especially that flower man'

Binemil: 'What should I do now? For all these years, I have dreamed to explore what is hiding behind that gate. Now I have nothing to dream. I should jump into that heat pit'

Kid: 'No, don't be like that. Be with me, these people, and all the new people coming here. Why dream big? Enjoy what you have'

Binemil: 'I feel like I am nothing! Just a big piece of flesh and bones, a giant man who keeps digging the ground so much that it created a whole root system under his feet. I feel like I am a part of this mountain. Leave me kid, enjoy your blissful future'

Kid: 'Stop thinking too much. You know the importance of being nothing? You can have a peaceful life. And you are not nothing, you farmed food for centuries here without expecting a reward. Think about that. You transformed this hard structure into a fertile land that can feed a whole planet of people'

Binemil stopped his worry speech and joined the Kid. Together, they formed groups with the new people and others. With nothing to worry about, Binemil became a people pleaser, did hard labour willingly to create special crops. He became the crowd favourite with his thousand-year-old narratives about his visits to the Gateman, and the evolution Midtory had. Thirty years passed, the Kid turned into an Adult. One day, the Adult proposed,

Adult: 'Binemil. What is your opinion on meeting the Gateman for one last time?'

Binemil: 'If you say so. You go first'

Adult: 'No, I don't want to. I want to be here. You take a try'

Binemil went to the top, the same old setup welcomed him. The Gateman sensed Binemil's presence, came out.

Gateman: 'I thought you were dead. Disappointed. I admire your skill of turning more ugly year after year'

Binemil remained calm, he was not getting angry. Instead, he kept looking at the ground as if he was ashamed of himself.

Gateman: 'Oh. Mockery? Your time is over. Go and waste another year. Enjoy'

Binemil nodded his head, gently turned back and walked...

Gateman: 'How dare you walk away like that! Who gave you permission to disobey my commands. Do ten frog jumps now!'

Binemil did ten frog jumps without hesitation nor questioning the Gateman. Binemil's face had that expression of grief even before he came to meet the Gateman.

Gateman: 'What is my age?'

Binemil: 'I don't know. Am over a thousand'

Gateman: 'How dare you speak back to me. You have the courage to curse me? I am sending you into the pits of flame. Get out!'

Binemil turned away and started his descend. But his walk was interrupted by Gateman's call for him. Binemil looked back, the doors to the next mysterious location were opened, Gateman hand signalled Binemil to pass the gate. But Binemil kept his descent going and joined the Adult and his beloved community' (narration ends)

Me: 'What kind of a story was that? What happened to Binemil, did he forget what he was doing or where he was?'

One: 'No, Binemil had no intention to succeed in the interview with the Gateman. He did it to test his own progression'

Me: 'What progression? Life? He had the chance to progress, if only he walked into the new location. What happened?'

One: 'Do you remember the time when the Kid lied to Binemil about what was hiding behind the mysterious gate?'

Me: 'Yes, I do remember. What about that? And I do remember Binemil becoming a dreamless man after hearing that lie'

One: 'And he started to enjoy the small things he had missed in his thousand years of living. He became a big brother to all the new and old residents of Midtory'

Me: 'Existential dilemma, isn't it?'

One: 'Yes. The fact that humanity is always after the hunt for the next step towards something, be it physical or not, they prefer to progress forever'

Me: 'What is wrong with that? We can't stay primitive forever, can we? And if they don't work, they will be put into the box of sloths, right?'

One: 'Do you call Binemil a sloth? And I never said humanity should stay primitive forever'

Me: 'Binemil was great. Please explain your last answer, Master'

One: 'You see, Binemil was after his dream of entering the mysterious gate, and for a thousand years he received insults from the cruel Gateman. And it was after him getting slipped into the infamous existential dilemma, he succeeded in surpassing the Gateman's crooked interview'

Me: 'Ok. I get it now. His dream-driven mind was filled with aggression and pride; thus, he was unable to cope with the Gateman's insults. But he threw harsh words at Binemil, he had no chance'

One: 'He had the chance to question him, correct him. Why didn't he? Word for word, not sword. Instead, he drilled his anger into the hard ground'

Me: 'So, what happened to him after getting into the dilemma thing? He forgot his mind, his pride, his anger?

One: 'Yes. He did. And we will also like him if it happens to us. Let me explain that further, Humans, the moment they are born, will get placed in a web of things like their identity, education, relations, religion, culture, future, and the only thing left for them is to enact the web structure because, failing to do so would label them as dumb and useless. Pride, Envy, Anger etc. Joins them to help them win the web. This web varies from region to region, country to country...'

Me: 'So, Binemil finally cut his web, and was freed. Entered the dilemma, didn't know what to live for, the purpose whatever. And that resulted in him getting freed from all the negative emotions associated with the web. Am I right, Master?'

One: 'Yes... I know what you are still concerned about. If freed from the web, will humanity become aimless and lazy, that could result in their extinction. Am I right?'

Me: 'Exactly. Life will become a burden if we have nothing to do. This is exactly what I thought when I spent my days inside the bottle after my last narration work'

One: 'Was that the final part of that Trilogy thing?'

Me: 'Yes, and the author did promise me that he would give me a spot in his own built "Relax centre" thing, but I was teleported back to one glass bottle placed inside a cardboard box filled with artistic drawings. And I did feel the so-called E-dilemma thing, I would have killed myself if I had the tools'

One: 'Luckily, you are still alive, and what did you do during that alone time?'

Me: (silence) 'I thought about myself, my life, even though I only know about my life from the words of a fiction writing Author, who seriously thought that Absurdity was a great technique'

One: 'Leave the Author alone, please. Now, what were the things you have found about yourself, from your self-thinking?'

Me: 'I found a lot of things about my personality and was surprised to know that I felt envy of the Author for his ability to control me. But I thanked him for selecting me as the narrator when I was trapped inside the bottle thing, alone'

One: 'Ok. Human life should not be a complex race to achieve something. The first thing that a human being should do, when they acquire the ability to think, is to think about their own self. Their interests, strengths and weaknesses, fears, favourite games, hobbies, people etc. And only after that try to study other people's life, from books, other medias and observing, not spying. But, they should never imitate the others. Instead, they should analyse the good and bad qualities they have'

Me: 'But master, how can they know about what is good and bad? What are qualities?'

One: 'From schools, parents, relatives, books. What kind of question was that? I was not talking about infants! And I once again quote "Humans should do when they acquire the ability to think" it varies from person to person'

Me: 'What if their parents are busy, relatives are enemies and have no access to books. How then?'

One: 'Schools. Children spend most of their conscious time in schools, the perfect space for acquiring wisdom'

Me: 'Not happening. Schools don't teach the subject called human. What about now?'

One: 'Then they should, that's it. Just like exercising helps the body to get rid of harmful toxins, thinking about oneself can get rid of mind toxins that will make people commit Sin. By keeping our mind engaged with good thoughts, it can defend against the Devil that will prey on the idle mind. Ever since Binemil was manipulated by the Kid's lie, he had nothing else to think about other than the well-being of his community, because all his negative emotions left him. The place Midtory was like a prison, people who committed sinful deeds were given plenty of time to think about themselves, which was the reason behind their entrapment there.'

Me: 'Modern humans are always busy, and even if they have free time, there exists plenty of other things to waste their time on instead of thinking about themselves. And the irony is that they curse others for their own depression'

One: 'Humans ignore the fact that life is short and have no problem ignoring the good moments to run after the recipe for immortality, to reshape planets and organisms, to reprogram people's mind. All for what? Humans are not happy; they have no peace. Let them think about themselves, but they themselves are the ones responsible for that'

Me: 'Master, morning has arrived. Enjoy teaching these fools'

(silence)

EIGHT

SACRED DEBATE: PART THREE

Teacher: 'Ok. New round. Your team's turn, Master'
One: 'Kids, go on'
Kid: 'The necessity of being Humble'
Student: 'Sorry, was that a question? And what does Humble mean?'
Teacher: 'Humble means not having pride, not arrogant'
Parent: 'Pride is the worst, luckily I don't have it'
Student: 'You own four houses, and five cars, you are definitely prideful, stop playing nice!'
Parent: 'How do you know all that?'
Student: 'Not important. Master, does this man belongs to the pride category?'
One: 'Yes. The desire to own more earth is prideful. The selfish concern for the growth of one's own family tree in the upcoming centuries, is what makes a person crave for more earth and other possessions'
Parent: 'I don't need the whole Earth! I didn't even visit another country. Not a fan of becoming Earth's leader'

Teacher: 'What he meant by earth is Land, not the whole planet you dumb. Small letter e'

Parent: 'Oh, that makes sense. But there are people who have more than ten buildings to their name, what about them? I have only four. And I built them for my two sons'

Kid: 'Can't they live in one house?'

Parent: 'No, we all need privacy, married life needs privacy to work better. Everyone knows it'

Student: 'Master, this man is still holding on to the predator – prey system. What is wrong with this man?'

Student: 'And he is still boasting about the schedule that comes up with Marriage!'

One: 'Calm down sons, let him hold on to his beliefs, he is fifty plus, it is difficult to alter all the beliefs he has accumulated over all these years. The most important thing is that you should be different. And I think we are a little off our main topic. Go on'

Student: 'Sorry Master, I am just wondering that if pride is the ultimate cause of alienation? Please enlighten us Master'

One: 'Good thinking dear. Alienation is one's personal choice. And pride is the main reason for many other struggles that keeps punching humanity down'

Student: 'Please explain, Master'

One: 'Pride causes Betrayal, Depression along with Alienation. The major factor of pride is that it is synonymous with selfishness. To become Humble is not an easy task. The ability to understand how other people feel is the first step, must spend a long time on this subject. People are so good at hiding their struggles, this hiding is also caused by Pride'

Teacher: 'Pride, Pride, Pride! What is this?'

One: 'Calm down son. Pride made you yell at me, don't you see? You felt like being ignored in front of your students, and that feeling woke up your pride'

(silence)

One: 'First, let's start with the sacred quality, Humble'

Kid: 'Being Humble means not taking pride in one's own skills and fortune, or at least not showing off'

Teacher: 'What was that explanation? Not showing off'

Student: 'I know what he meant, to show Pride, there exists luxurious materials and activities, created only for this showing purpose. If the pride-full people were to not let loose themselves inside this circle, and instead use their extra luxury wealth to help small businesses and other people who need help'

One: 'That's a good explanation son. The main reason for people opting to spend their unwanted fortune off by buying items labelled as luxury but no use, is because of the lack of solidarity. Solidarity helped humanity achieve great heights, overcome man-made destructions. And the cease of it has paved way for the rise of selfishness and pride, which made them less generous'

Student: 'Master, please explain about the connection Pride has with other problems'

One: 'Ok. But first, what is Alienation? The reason?'

Teacher: 'Being alone. People opt to be alone to focus more on their self. And I do appreciate that, because it helps to build one's career'

One: 'What is it's connection with Depression, and what is your opinion on the rise of depression?'

Teacher: 'Depression is the feeling arising from thinking about getting ignored by others, the feeling of getting rejected in life, and having no hope for the future. Being alone can increase Depression because the person won't be getting any consolation'

Student: 'Master, what makes people betray others?'

One: 'Son, your face gives me the impression that you have once fallen victim to a treacherous incident... No need to cry dear, it is painful, and that is why Treachery is considered the deadliest Sin. Once again, Selfishness cause betrayals, the greedy need to outperform other people at any cost makes one think about this deadliest Sin. Stop crying son...'

Student: 'Sorry Master, I was betrayed once, by my best friend. He and I were friends from second grade; we always spent time together. And when we joined college for our graduation, he started loving one of our classmates. She was very pretty and arrogant, she didn't enjoy me talking with him. They started ignoring me from then. And during one of the university exams, when I was cheating with my own micro note materials, the exam squad came into the class and caught my friend's lover who was copying the answer materials made by me, but my friend announced that he saw me threw a bit of paper around, and angrily announced me as the cheater. Her fake cry was enough to satisfy the exam squad; I was debarred for three years!' (angry cry)

One: 'Don't worry son, focus on your talents, never be worried about some paper exams. The real exam is happening inside you, speak to yourself, let the Wrath out of your way by turning it into self-energy. And always keep in mind that you are a human being who has gone through the deadliest of Sin. You can now withstand anything, think of anything and you will achieve it. Stop crying'

Student: 'Thank you Master. I will not cry anymore. But why did he betray me for a girl he knew for two months, it is this question that keep confusing me. No, I don't care about that anymore. I am the survivor; nothing can stop me'

One: 'Why are you laughing, mister Parent?'

Parent: 'You think that was a betrayal? I have one better. Two years back, my friend went to a road trip and had an accident. He lost control because of the foggy weather, hit a rock. He was injured and was taken to the nearest hospital. He was discharged the same day, nothing serious. But the real issue was that when he went to the accident spot to retrieve his belongings, all he could find was the Car... His wallet, phone, bag, laptop, even the soft drink bottle was stolen. He later found out that his bank account was emptied, and most of his stolen cards were used to get hefty loans by the thieves'

Student: 'What kind of devils were they! Master, can we call them human beings?'

One: 'Relax son. In a world filled with competition of pride and other deadly Sins, Wrath makes anyone brave and evil enough to do unimaginable things, and every human being has Wrath enshrined inside their blood for free...

(silence)

People find pride in everything, beauty, fame, money, even in the firelighters they carry. It makes a person devoid of empathy and sympathy, making the person not care about anyone's feelings'

Student: 'Master, I didn't get any attention from my classmates, is that because I am not good looking? Does pride exist in beauty?'

One: 'Yes, my dear. Beauty does count as an object to pride for'

Student: 'Is that why good-looking people are at the peak inside the marriage market?'

One: 'Why are you surprised, my dear? Beauty is not something limited to the infamous marriage market but to racial conflicts, stereotyping's, exploitations of different kinds'

Student: 'What should I do, Master? My family doesn't have the money to invest on beauty surgeries and products. Master, I know you have spoken against marriage ideology, but I want to marry. I don't have any close friends, I know you can understand my feeling'

One: 'Don't beat yourself my dear, focus on your talents, your skills. I know I have mentioned it for many times. You don't have to make a fake yawn mister parent, I get it. Child, you should stop worrying about such matters, you will find your perfect partner. Just remember that Wisdom beats everything. People who have true wisdom don't care for pride'

Teacher: 'When it comes to the marriage market, people prefer beauty over wisdom, because they can show off with their partner's beauty. No one is interested in creating a debate of wisdom like this boring one we are playing for a couple of days!'

One: 'Why are you getting angry son? If you want rest, please take some. I know it is almost night; I can understand your anger'

(silence)

All of them have gone to sleep except Master One, I wonder what he is made of.

Me: 'Master, are you alright? You look little worried'

One: 'Yes, the last discussion was not properly ended. That student is not feeling well'

Me: 'Don't worry about that Master. She will be alright. If I may, people marrying solely based on beauty, often lead a good successful life. I have seen photos and short video clips of them celebrating happiness'

One: 'What else should they do? Show depressive photos, videos of crying hard? You see, Relationship formed out of beauty is built on the foundation of pride. It is destined to stoop down one way or another, and when they fail, their pride will not allow them to open themselves to others'

Me: 'Oh, that's why there exist statements like, Marriage requires compromise, adjustment, understanding, forgiveness, tolerance etc. But why people consider Beauty as supreme?'

One: 'People assign sacred qualities to Beauty, without giving a second thought. Being beautiful is judged as having a good soul, and people crave to be with someone beautiful because they can pride themselves for getting matched with a good soul'

Me: 'That's a shameful assumption. It makes people waste their wealth and time on uplifting their beauty standards, and the worst part is that how this sacred assumption can make the less-beautiful guilty and depressed. What's up with that?'

One: 'I have already made my remarks on the whole marriage thing earlier. The pride that hangs around Beauty has turned the whole system into a market of objectification. Human beings are getting a price tag on themselves based on Beauty, and I do know there exists many other reasons for this price tag thing'

Me: 'Master, am getting frustrated with this whole debate. No offence. I should take some time off this. Will see you soon, Master. Please excuse me'

(silence)

(silence)

Oh, come on! Not the double silence! Can't I take some rest! Whatever, where is Master? Is he asleep? He is meditating? I must wake him up, can't let those pesky silence things ruin this work anymore. Master, wake up...

One: 'What's wrong, son? what is bothering you?'

Student: 'Master. It's me, the narrator. I forgot to ask you this last time, what was the actual reason behind the betrayal of that boy?'

One: 'Why are you dressed up like this? Where did you get this dress? Is everything alright?'

Me: 'Sorry to inform you sir, one of the male students took a walk through the snowfield last night, I found his body submerged inside the snow. Tried to save him, but he disappeared when I touched him, leaving only his uniform behind. I took it'

One: 'Ok. What do you want now?'

Me: 'Are you not worried about the death news?'

One: 'Don't worry about that, he will be alright. Just tell me what you want to know'

Me: 'I want to know about the betrayal, that poor boy his evil friend and his lover. Remember?'

One: 'Oh, that. Men seek pride in finding a mate, and according to the instinctual human theory, securing a perfect mate is a crucial achievement. That boy only had to put a slight amount of thought while deciding to betray his best friend for his mate'

Me: 'Ok. Am ready for the next story'

One: 'This will be the final story, because this work will be finished by tomorrow. Hope you understand'

Me: 'What! But this is barely hundred pages. And less entertaining. No offence'

One: 'None taken. This work is different; you will get your queries cleared at the end. Wait patiently'

Me: 'Ok Master. Please tell the final story'

NINE

MYTHIC TALE: PART THREE

One: 'Once upon a time, there was a village called Canoe, that was filled with happiness and prosperity. Rivers, Gardens, Farms, Pastures, Hills, and average sized buildings. Nymphs were seen there, and the mighty "Keith" was the sovereign guard of the village. It was rumoured that Keith was assigned by the Almighty lord. The Canoe village was free from corruption, and Keith was the reason behind it. He engaged in the villagers' personal affairs and offered best advice to them. All the people wore white robes irrespective of gender. Keith taught them how important the sacred values are and helped them in need. But the inevitable evilness was often formed in specific spots, Keith took care of them without mercy using his water sword, made of holy water.

People were not born there because getting intimate was not approved by Keith. He even created a four-page booklet containing the rules and advises regarding how to live in Canoe village, and one of the clauses clearly prohibited touching other people. New people came out of a mysterious door carved into the Hill, but the door couldn't be opened manually nor could see what was behind it. Keith welcomed them first and immediately handed them the booklet. Keith was also not a fan of private property; he built a limited number of buildings across the map to promote vagabonding. Thus, everyone was forced to live in random spots rather than sticking to one location. The inhabitants were required to do labour for five hours each day, but it was Keith with his magical powers, created the necessary food.

Keith was advised by the Almighty, to never let the people suffer the slightest. He made the five hours rule to not promote laziness, otherwise the labour was useless. Keith also created the rule of mandatory worship to God, but the people were fond of it anyway. Keith was not stubborn though he looked tough with his water sword, chest armour made of coconut husk, carved out rock helmet, and a skirt made of jackfruit skin for creating an aesthetic appeal. Keith was very happy to spend time with his people; he addressed them as his children. He created meetings and journeys purposefully to unite his children with the newcomers. The most peculiar thing about the Canoe village was that the inhabitants never aged, thus death was not there.

One day, a blue smoke appeared beside the river. Keith sensed the rise of the evil entity, went there to destroy it. Keith was surprised to find a fully grown evil thing, with sharp horns, standing inside the smoke. Keith took out his water sword, aimed for its head, but the entity fearlessly stared into Keith's eyes. Keith was stymied but he regained control shortly.

Keith: 'I am about to incinerate you, better luck next time'

Devil: 'Proceed, you dumb creature. Scapegoat the innocent'

Keith: 'Innocent! (laughs) Your kind is the destroyer of every bond, stop taking birth here!'

Devil: (laughs) 'I was not born but made, by your loving people living here. The sins they do, get accumulated here and there across this place, and this burden of sins float around and then join to form entities like me. Stop taking pride in your people's innocence. They are fooling you, fool!'

Keith: 'How dare you accuse my children! Get ready to feel the pain of my weapon'

Devil: 'What a loser! There is a crime happening right now. And you are here boasting about your children'

Keith: 'Stop lying you disgraceful thing. Prepare to die'

Devil: 'Am prepared, what is making you delay? You do know how crooked your people are, don't you?'

Keith: 'Stop blaming my people, they believe in only one thing, sharing is caring'

Devil: 'Are you referring to sharing one's wife to another one, what a mess is this place, kill me fast or else'

Keith: 'Or else what? You can do nothing'

Devil: 'You do fear that I can corrupt your people, don't you? And the answer is Yes. They are already corrupted, and with one touch of my fingers can turn them mad enough to cause trouble for your fancy sword. Fool!'

Keith: 'Prove it. If you can corrupt my people, I will set you free, but if you fail, you will be locked inside the Dungeon of Flames forever. And keep in mind, Death is far better than getting locked in the Dungeon for eternity'

Devil: 'Agreed. This won't take long. And to make this little spicier, I will not make my presence visible to your people. Just stay here and watch'

Devil walked into the village; Keith watched each movement of it. Devil was invisible to the residents, it first went to a crowded location, and then turned itself into a medium sized Diamond, bright as the moon. Keith made a scoff and dismissed its existence. The Devil remained there for a few hours but none of the people touched it. Finally, someone touched it. The Devil turned back into its true scary form, with an expression of victory on its face. But Keith was the one touched it.

Keith: 'It is night. Stop clowning around! Surrender and die?'

Devil: 'No, I will not. Give me another chance, I know how to defeat them'

Keith: 'You can take any number of chances, until you say "I Surrender" I won't end you. Have fun'

Devil: 'You will regret telling me this'

Morning arrived. People started their daily routine of wandering and chanting prayers here and there. Devil saw a group of people surrounding a small hill, and it took the chance. It turned into a mirror and attached into a carved area of the hill. Soon, they found the mirror, observed themselves, made jokes and laughed around, and left. After a few hours, Keith made his entrance, once again he had that scoff painted across his face. Keith styled himself looking in the mirror, gave it a gentle tap and left without saying anything but "Idiot". Night came, the Devil stopped his acting and went back to the riverside to think more carefully about its next move.

Next morning, Keith woke up the Devil and ordered it to start its actions because it was fun to watch. Devil became furious, carefully located a less crowded place near the valley. Only a few people were there, debating about the existence of evil forces. Meanwhile, the real Devil turned into a fallen log filled with small sharp branches. And as soon as the little crowd started moving, the fake log did a few rolls and grabbed one of the women's robes with one of its sharp branches. The woman fell to the ground, naked! But one of the men picked up the robe from the fake branch, dressed her back, and they walked away like nothing happened there.

(Branch snapping noise followed by screams, the devil transformed back to its original form)

Devil: 'Please don't hurt me. You gave me your word'

Keith: 'This beating is for you hurting my child. If you hurt my children ever again!'

Devil: 'I am sorry, I won't hurt them again! I swear! Am just an evil thing'

Next day, the Devil located a steep mountain, and people were standing on top of it. Instead of climbing it, the Devil turned into a massive sized bed, tempting enough to make anyone drop dead on it. But the people had no interest to spend their time on it except some of them used the sides to sit. The Devil patiently waited till night. Keith made a furious jump onto the bed, almost breaking it in half. Devil turned into his original image, ran away. Keith couldn't contain his mighty laughter. That night, the Devil met Keith.

Devil: 'Sir, I surrender. I accept my defeat. But before you kill me, I want to show my gratitude to your innocent children. Let me cook a grand meal for them, please'

Keith: (laughs) 'Fine, take this magic wand, it has the power to create any food item you want. And prepare to die next day'

The Devil took the magic wand and walked to the river side, it spawned culinary ingredients left and right. It spent the whole night creating a wide variety of delicious looking dishes. In the morning, mouth-watering aroma filled the whole place and attracted the people to take a look at it. Keith encouraged his children to consume the food and be happy. They started eating the food and stopped eating after consuming a good amount of food. The problem was that there remained an abundance of food still.

Keith: 'Why did you make this much food?'

Devil: 'I am evil, I love more'

Keith: 'Understandable. I can't let food go to waste. My children, eat as much as you can, wasting food is sinful'

Devil: (whispered) 'Famous last words'

Keith's children rushed into the scene, with more aggression this time. They stuffed their mouth with plenty of food, enjoyed the joy of satisfying their palate. Keith's face bloomed with happiness, he changed his focus to the Devil, took out his Water sword.

Keith: 'Time has finally arrived. Any last words'

Devil: 'Look over there! That man is hurting that young lady'

Keith: (gasps) 'What is happening! Hey you, stop hurting her. How dare you attack her!'

Him: 'Who are you to control us, you sick old freak? We are not your toys!'

Keith: 'You too, my child...'

The Devil kept laughing aggressively. Keith and his children bowed their head in shame. Out of nowhere, a bright light appeared on the sky along with heavy lightning strikes. The Devil was struck with one massive lightning, incinerated it instantly. And another strong lightning bolt opened a wide hole on the ground; it formed a deep pit with hot fumes pumping out of it.

Light: 'Everyone except Keith, jump into that pit now'

The people remained carelessly. Suddenly, a huge tornado swirled them all up and dropped them into the deep heat pit. Keith was the only one standing there, and he was still in bowed position.

Light: 'Look up Keith. See what you have done?'

Keith: 'I never thought my children would get corrupted by that devil. I was corrupted by my own pride. Forgive me lord, please send me to the Dungeon'

Light: 'Even Adam and Eve couldn't do it, what made you think your people could? You already lost when you accepted the bet with the Devil. I have given you that water sword to not make bet with anyone'

Keith: 'I seriously thought that my children would never get troubled by some food! I should have stopped them from eating more food than they needed. I let them have fun with their palate since they wouldn't be hurting anyone because it was excess food, and would have gone to waste, so it wouldn't be classified under the Sin, Gluttony'

Light: 'Gluttony is not about eating other people's food! Eating more food will create a stimulus inside the human mind, that will then crave for more food, and over time, this craving can transfer into other things like materialistic things, sexual cravings, thirst for violence'

Keith: 'Forgive me, my lord. I didn't know that. Punish me...'

Keith was sent to the Dungeon of Flames, and a new protector was assigned to the village Canoe' (narration ends)

Me: 'Master, what was that Gluttony thing? I don't quite understand. How is eating food connected to other serious deadly Sins. I know that being gluttonous can be harmful to other people because the gluttonous person can cause food shortage'

One: 'You know there is plenty of food, then how can a few gluttonous people cause food shortage?'

Me: 'Master, what I meant was that, let's put it this way, like if I were running a hotel business, and at night, the balance food was given away to the poor and homeless people, but if some gluttonous people ate the extra food, it would lead to no excess food, and thus the people dependent on that become thrashed. How is my answer? Some hotel owners do this, I have heard of them'

One: 'Your explanation is good. But it not the actual definition of the Sin Gluttony. You see, food is essential for survival, and giving respect to food automatically makes a person not gluttonous. The person who has no respect for food eats more, and this non-respect attitude will transfer into their lives as well. They will become Greedier in every aspect of their life'

Me: 'So, controlling food can save people from not only a variety of diseases but committing sins also? Dieting should be made mandatory then, right master?'

One: 'Nothing can be forced. People won't obey forced rules, instead they should be made aware of the issues. Talking about food and hunger, the hunger for food is the primary hunger of human beings. And only then comes the hunger for power, pride, lust, wealth etc. And if a person gets gluttonous, they will completely ignore its primary position and moves it to the secondary position. The modern era is highly fixated on food industry, and that promotes Gluttonous behaviour among people. People are eating more than enough food just for the sake of happiness, but they are making themselves sad in the process. And there are millions of people who are getting starved still, the horrible irony!'

Me: 'Thank you master. Still few hours left for morning, please take some rest'
(silence)

TEN

THE ULTIMATE SACRED DEBATE

Morning's here. Debate has started.

Student: 'Master, can you please explain how dangerous it is to use drugs like Cigarette and Alcohol?'

One: 'Am not going to talk about the damage that drugs will do to a person's body. The overall invention of drugs did unthinkable damage to humanity'

Parent: 'People take drugs to ease their tensions and to forget the horrible embarrassing events they suffered. To get Peace'

Teacher: 'As long as the drug user does not cause any trouble to other people, it is a personal choice. People who use drugs, take pleasure in getting exhausted and out of consciousness. But they are indeed exchanging their life years for it'

One: 'Why do people opt to get exhausted and unconscious willingly? that's the real danger'

Parent: 'Life is stressful, only a man who has no family and does not need to worry about taxes can speak negative on drugs'

One: 'Ok mister parent. If life is stressful, then try to make it not stressful, don't rely on getting exhausted from pesky drugs!'

Parent: 'You are so naive, get a taste of real life'

One: 'Stop defending drugs. Getting wasted with drugs is a Sin that you are committing against your own self. Instead, you must focus on converting your energy into other endeavours, that can bring goodness to you and the whole humanity'

Parent: 'Blah blah blah... Stop using the word humanity, please! My happiness is my top priority, am not working for the benefit of every human being, understand. Ninety percent of people are like me, what is the need of thinking about humanity before taking every action! It is not possible; I can't even bring goodness to my family or myself'

Kid: 'Calm down Sir. Master was talking about drugs, he wants you to think about humanity before using drugs, not before every action. Each human being is bestowed with divine energy from their birth, and it is the reason behind the prosperity of humanity and the world. Master was talking about that divine energy, and he is advising you and all the drug users, to not waste it on drugs because this energy is key to uplift one's skills and abilities'

Student: 'Master, are you proposing the idea of humanity working for every hour and day. I remember that you have objected this proposal earlier... What's up with that?'

One: 'I did not make that proposal; I was advocating to not get lost with the help of drugs. And speaking about your concern, what did you mean by using the term, Working?'

Student: 'Like we already discussed, working is the use of physical and intellectual energy of a person to the betterment of themselves, their family, and humanity. And what I was proposing is that we need time to leisure and relax as well'

One: 'What are the leisure things you like to do?'

Student: 'I like to go on journeys, adventures, visit the museum, watch a movie, eat in a fancy restaurant. Am sure those are not classified as working'

One: 'Why not? If you go on a journey, you are spreading your energy out into the paths you have travelled, and this spread-out energy will then get absorbed by the surroundings. And if you watch a movie, you are spending your energy by analysing it, and at the same time, you are supporting the art form. Wasting your divine energy on drugs is disrespectful'

Parent: 'What about sleeping, Is that a waste of energy?'

One: 'Definitely not. Sleeping is necessary to heal your body, the divine energy is something related to your soul not your physical body, which is just a carrier of soul'

Parent: 'Oh my! Am getting tired hearing these metaphysical overload'

One: 'It is getting dark, let's stop debating and get some rest'

Parent: 'It's been three days since we got trapped in here, how long we must wait! Please let us go'

Student: 'Maybe you want to go, we don't. We want to stay here with you Master. We need your guidance'

Parent, 'Stop praising this man, he is trying to trap us all in his secret den. Mister, we can't tolerate anymore'

One: 'Calm down mister parent, before we part, let's play one final round. Do you believe in God?'

Parent: 'I do. We all do. God created us, and God is everywhere protecting all of us'

One: 'What made you believe in God?'

Parent: 'It is because of God's blessings, I got my job, and my family. God is behind all my success'

Teacher: 'Your hard work and dedication made you succeed, not God. Science is the truth. Master, prove me wrong?'

Student: 'How could you say that? Scientists are still not able to decipher some of the complex aspects of human body. Do you have any respect for the one who created it?'

Teacher: 'How can you be sure that God has created the world?'

Student: 'Sure the scientists are not the creators'

Teacher: 'The big bang theory, all happened in a friction of time. Are we clear?'

Student: 'It is just a theory! People are worshipping God in every part of the world. How can you not acknowledge that?'

One: 'Please calm down. Let's not argue about God. What is your opinion on worshipping God?'

Teacher: 'People just want to put all their mistakes and wrong deeds on top of faith and God, instead of acknowledging their sins confidently and bettering themselves. They excuse their struggles by calling it God's plan. Instead of wasting time worshipping God, they should work hard'

One: 'What does God symbolise? Any thoughts?'

(silence)

Parent: 'Our protector, fortune giver?'

One: 'God is an embodiment of all the sacred values such as Love, Kindness, Humble, Merciful etc. Not touched by any of the deadly Sins. To worship God, we should worship God's qualities. Treating God like a wishing well is not worshipping. Human beings can never perfect themselves like God, but they should try, nonetheless. Only a very few of human beings have conquered at least half of the deadly sins'

Student: 'Master, you have promised to answer one of my questions about Mercy, at the end of the last round, I believe but not sure. I can't recollect what my exact question was'

One: 'I do remember that my child. Your question was about whether human beings are born with sacred values or evilness. The answer is, both, and that's why children are innocent and are at high risk of getting their innocence exploited by evils, resulting in them taking a slide to the bad side. The family, the place where a child is born, and the sacred qualities exhibited by those around the child, make the child better. But, on the other hand, if a child is born to a careless, less quality parents, the child's bad side will take dominance'

Teacher: 'Come on Master, you can't escape every time with a paradox! Why are human beings born with the best and the worst side all together? Why aren't they born with only the best side?'

One: 'That's an excellent question son. If humans were born with only their best side, they would have never progressed and might have gone extinct. For the perfect harmony, the sacred and the not sacred qualities need to be present in humanity, at different rates. I will explain why... Love is a sacred quality, meanwhile Lust is not. Love is the binding force that helps to maintain human lives. Every human does possess Love, but some fail to expose it because they won't make the effort to find another human to offer it to. They will then offer their love to other objects, animals. Hence, without Lust, human beings will not be able to reproduce and might have gone extinct long before like every other animal would have in the absence of Lust.

The crucial thing is always having the wisdom to understand the reason behind every thought made inside a person's mind by themselves. Most of the population are not interested in analysing their own rollercoaster of thoughts because of their addiction to wild technologies and the stress that modern life is full of'

Teacher: 'We have to put food on our tables. Making notes on the millions of random thoughts won't provide money!'

One: 'I understand your emotion but, that's not an excuse. You do know how much leisure time you spend on other activities, spending a few minutes on yourself is not too much to ask for'

Student: 'Don't mind him Master, please continue your explanation of the sacred qualities coexisting with the evils'

Teacher: 'Who are you? I haven't seen you before'

Student: 'Oh, have you forgot your students? "Master, it's me the narrator, please continue" (narrator whispered)

One: 'Ok son... Mercy is a sacred quality, meanwhile Wrath is not. Human beings are born with Mercy, but Wrath never allows a person to give it straight forward. Wrath analyses the scenario inside this person's mind and questions their mind about what will be its response if the same Mercy seeking incident would have happened to this person. And this analysis will create a sense of guilt for giving the culprit Mercy. This occurs because the victim never has made a similar mistake to test their overall Mercy give and take ability. But if humans were born without Wrath, they will never learn the value of Mercy, and when they make errors, because of the unique flaws found in every human being that makes them imperfect, without Wrath, they will never feel much about their error. Wrath helps a person's consciousness to get better, the crucial thing here is the ability to control and suppress Wrath. And understanding why we feel it...

(silence)

Moving on. Industrious is a scared quality, but Sloth is not. The industrious quality helps humanity to progress and advance; this quality has helped them found out secrets hiding beyond the planet Earth. But too much industrious is never healthy, because this can lead to uncontrolled experiments and studies that will trouble the natural habitat. The peace received from Laziness helps them reconnect with other sacred values. The crucial thing to remember is that both Industrious and Laziness need to work in a perfect split, because if Laziness overtakes the other, it can make people less industrious, and they will then settle for an utopian style life, where everyone does farming works and lives the same life.

(silence)

Again, moving on. Being Humble is a sacred quality, but Pride is not. Being Humble to other people can drastically improve their mental health, even if they were struggling from the most painful events possible. But Pride, on the other hand, keeps a person self-motivated for bettering themselves. Though it sounds selfish, it is necessary for a human being to understand their self. Although being fully humble is not dangerous. Pride helps a person to become little more competent, in a good way. To be precise, Pride helps a person to become more industrious. Balance is the key; too much pride can make the person selfish enough to desire the whole world under their arms.

(silence)

Once again, moving on. Kindness is a sacred quality, but Envy is not. Like we have mentioned earlier, being Kind to a person, is the most important quality a human being should have. There is no reason for being Unkind. Like all animals, Human beings' life cycle is also limited, and Life is not just a race to finish somehow. The foremost thing a person can wish for is Peace. But there exist many obstacles to pass through for achieving it, and if a person is Kind, this person will have peace, and they will also help others get it. Kindness paves way for selfless acts. Now, Envy makes a person to judge themselves, and it makes pity take growth in them. They will even pity themselves. If a person is Kind but does not have the means or knowledge to help others, that person will suffer themselves for their inability to help the people who need help... Envy helps a person to study other people, to make themselves better. But too much Envy makes them powerful enough to destroy the person who is envied.

(silence)

Ok. Moving on... Being Philanthropic (generous) is a good quality, but Greedy is not. Philanthropy makes a person to care for other human beings, not just giving charity but by carrying forward missions pertaining to different sectors such as medical, science, anthropology, humanities etc. Philanthropy makes a person motivated and dedicated. Greediness helps a person to maintain good focus for achieving difficult milestones. Greediness makes a person think that everything this person does, is getting evaluated, and will be considered for the nomination of some kind of priceless eternal reward.

(silence)

Ok. Am done with my speech on the coexistence of qualities. Anything else?

Parent: 'Get us out of here. Take us to our homeland'

Teacher: 'Master, are you going to make a portal to our place? Am excited'

Student: 'I am not going back to my home, Master, please let me stay here for the rest of my life'

About half of the students opted to stay with Master. Meanwhile, the others are thrilled to exit this wretched place. The teacher tried his best to withdraw the master supporting students but failed.

One: 'There is nothing I can do. I don't possess magical powers, forgive me for giving hope to all of you'

Parent: 'What! How dare you fool us! We won't tolerate a moment here. Come people, let's go, make haste'

Teacher: 'Yes, let's go students, we are brave. We will get to our homeland soon. Make haste'

The ignorant crew started their slow parade, have managed to reach very far, but they are still unable to locate a road. And now they have decided to get back to Master's place, but the footmarks on the snowy ground have disappeared. They don't know what to do, what to follow! Panic mode has set in; they ran bewildered but not even one of them managed to find Master's cave house. They all became exhausted and fell into the snowy depths, disappeared after a few minutes.

Ok, time to get back to Master's cave... I have been flying for almost an hour, still can't find his cave. What is happening? Is this the end? I am sure I will never find Master and his cave ever again. I can't believe how could anyone put an end to a book in this manner. There is nothing interesting, just repetitive sentences filled with unrealistic and not practical advises. What's up with that? Is anyone going to give a try at least? Am asking you, my readers! Are you going to experiment with the theories explained in this book? Highly unlikely...

No, I am not being a negative shade here. The fact of the matter is, every human being (modern) knows about good and bad, and the consequences of following the bad, but they still do it. For example, they know about the fact that without doing exercise, they will become unhealthy. And without doing work, they can't earn money. They even know that smoking kills, but they are happy to smoke a mouthful of cigar butts. I feel wasted! What is up with my fate? I thought this work would bring something exciting to me, never... Whoa! what is happening? I can't see... I am blind? Green mists! I am getting teleported to some place...

ELEVEN

THE HANDBOOK EXPERIMENT

I got my vision back. Am standing in front of a gate, in the middle of a paddy field. This gate opens into a mysterious four walled garden place. The walls are made of thick tree shavings, and the gate is not locked. Funny thing is, I can't turn invisible and because of that, can't fly. The paddy field has the stickiest mud, impossible to cross it. Without anything to do, I made my entrance into the walled structure, this is not a garden! The first thing caught my eyes is one glass structure that contains something invisible, and it is screaming. I think it is the bright light aka soul of Fiction. I went closer to the structure and made my presence known to it.

Me: 'Hello, is anybody in here? What is this place?'

It: (painful screaming) 'Run! Go away or prepare to be damned'

Me: 'What! Who are you? I can't go anywhere; this place is a labyrinth. I must return to the plot, have an incomplete story to complete. Maybe it has finished, and even if it hasn't, I don't want to endure it anymore!'

It: 'Oh, you are a narrator. Have you done any mistake? Said bad things about your work?'

Me: 'I did nothing wrong. It is a bad work, just some advice and stupid replies. What a mess! Am sure no one can withstand the craziness!'

It: 'You should not have said that! What kind of a moron are you! you know who I am and for what reason am I in here?'

Me: 'Soul of someone crazy enough to be imprisoned?'

It: 'I am the soul of fiction; I am imprisoned for breaking the laws of non-fiction'

Me: 'Why did you do that? You know what, I was also working in that kind of a work. The story of a king called Cadevar! Nonsense...'

It: 'Wait what! Are you the narrator of the philosophy work? Master One and the college tour group. Teachings of the scared values?'

Me: 'Yes, I am. What kind of a work is that, right? Sorry, how did you end up inside this structure? Who is more powerful than you? Am I in danger?'

It: 'Absolutely. You are inside the den of the Soul of the Universe. And I am punished for including the story of Cadevar into the work you have narrated' (screams in agony)

Me: 'When will you be released from this prison thing?'

It: 'Don't know (screams) Aaahhh... Go away... Go'

I don't know what to do, the gate has closed. What is this place? This is more mysterious than anything I have ever seen. I am surprised to find a place more absurd than the weird locations I have travelled through in the last part of that trilogy thing. This looks like a temple, there is one small building, enough to fit two people, standing in the middle. There is no soil, but twisted roots scattered all the way around this four-walled temple. I found a small glass box filled with sparkling dust! Can't open it. But then I found a metal box that can be opened with my limited strength... (thud!)

(intense breathing) Oh my... I believe it is hell inside that box... There is no other explanation I can give. I tried to open the silver and the gold boxes, but they can't be opened. And now there is only one more box to try my luck, the building that looks like a big box. To cause more trouble, it can be opened! I am scared but it might be the only escape plan for me. Slowly opened the door... Closed the door but am still outside. Yes, no escape for me, and don't get angry with me readers, I will tell you what I saw... I believe it was the Universe, with Planets, floating debris, Stars, Galaxies...

Anyway, I have decided to take a look at the small glass box filled with sparkling dust, of different colours. Opened it, picked one of the sparkling things. Sure, this is not a dusty thing, but one tiny ball of violet light. I don't know how I am able to hold it. While observing it more closely, the unexpected has happened! The bead of light dissolved into my skin, and I am now experiencing some mind trauma... Am getting sick... Headache. Something is getting pumped into my mind...

(silence)

(intense breathing) It is happening! I have a new story in my mind that I should narrate to relieve the burden off my mind. Finally, I am going to be an author and a narrator. Eyes closed, slowed my breathing, narration is starting, I was transferred into the plot location. There is a line, a queue of naked human beings, on a narrow bridge connecting the entrance to the exit, of a huge dome painted in the colour of flame. There is a royal chair on the left side of the exit door, and a man of high profile is sitting on it, but he is fully covered with golden clothes. I know my hero is standing in this queue, but don't know how to spot him... After careful observation of the queue people, I saw a man who is different from the others.

He looks bewildered, scared, and keeps running his eyes all around the dome. Now that I have found my hero, turned my attention to the entity on the chair, what is happening there? Some people are walking out through the exit door, some people have disappeared inside a cluster of sparkling smoke, and finally some people are getting thrown into the unknown depths under the bridge. I am not interested in the talks happening around the chair, I waited patiently for my heroes' turn. But he is a little behind the queue, and I don't want to ruin this story with more silence.

I flew past the chair to see what is hiding behind the exit door, there are altars decorated in flowers, white rocks with polished top, small stream of water flowing all around the little structures, constantly making a sweet ripple noise effect, clear white sky, people here and there spending their time taking care of the beautiful flowering plants. I am sure there is plenty more to explore, but the problem is that I can't enter through the transparent exit door, it's like some mysterious force stopping me from entering there. Anyway, my hero is now only behind a couple of others. The entity asked them a few questions and let them walk out of the exit door. My hero's turn has arrived, finally.

Entity: 'Shenen, I can't let you in no matter what. Any last words before getting dropped down into the depths?'

Shenen: 'I want to enter there, please give me a chance to prove my worth, I have changed'

Entity: 'You are strongly accused of being unkind to your fellow beings, you made them suffer'

Shenen: 'Suffer? I have never once raised my hands at anyone'

Entity: 'You did with words, expressions and your behaviour. And I bet you can't survive a day without acting unkind'

Shenen: 'I acknowledge that I harmed others with my words, only because I didn't know words are powerful enough to hurt others. And I accept the bet'

Entity: 'What if you lose?'

Shenen: 'Lock me in the depths for eternity, just give me my chance of redemption'

Entity: 'Ok. You will now be sent to an anonymous location, and your challenge is to be kind to everyone for twenty-four hours'

Green mist encircled Shenen, I went inside the mist. Both of us are spawned in the middle of an empty street, early morning I believe. But am invisible and can get away from the plotline whenever I want. Luckily, Shenen is not naked but excited, he checks on himself, finds a handbook along with a pocket watch inside one of his pant pockets. Shenen realises that the coat he is wearing is not removable, and he is sweating from all sides because of the hot weather. There is something I forgot to mention, the backside of his coat has an inscription, it says, "I am a professional helper sent from the Sky, meet me for Help. Thy trouble shall be cured"

Shenen does not know that his coat has an inscription. He takes out the handbook and reads it. And it is filled with statements that he can use to help the people who need help. The first heading it has is Mercy, followed by some key points.

The ability to forgive people

Agreeing with the fact that a person is not a master of all traits, mistakes are often caused from their lacking some traits

Being good to elders, the seeds of past, knowledge may differ but always give respect to their age

Wisdom makes all equal, it is the unwise who mocks a person's personal beliefs

Wisdom goes through a variety of changes when a person becomes old

A person shouldn't argue that their wisdom is greater than others, it is prideful, always try to be a Kid who craves to learn from other people

Offering a single smile, listening to their queries, not showing off oneself etc. can lighten up people's mind if they are in a sad frame

Shenen takes out his pocket watch chained to his pant pocket, it is not a regular watch but a timer for Shenen, and now it shows "23:34" and each time he takes the watch out, a robotic voice announces the time (Twenty-three hours and thirty-three minutes left) Shenen is bewildered, he doesn't know what to do, he decides to take a walk. The street turned alive, Shenen is getting noticed by the passerby people. He keeps memorising the bullet points mentioned in the book but gets interrupted by a young man. He looks exhausted, and he is dressed shabbily.

He: 'Hey man, I need your help. But I don't have anything to pay you, will you accept this watch?'

Shenen: 'Don't worry boy, I don't need anything, just tell me what you need help with'

He: 'I need to find a job. But the competition is very high here. Please help me sir'

Shenen excuses him and takes out his handbook, leafs through it and finds the sub-heading Unemployment in

'Sad' section. Shenen silently reads the section for a few times, he is trying to memorize them.

Shenen: 'What is your favourite thing to do? Do you have any skills?'

He: 'I don't know sir. I am a good driver, but this place is filled with taxis. Help me'

Shenen: 'What is the one skill you wish you had?'

He: 'How to seduce women, that will be an awesome skill to learn. And how to memorize thousand pages in a day'

Shenen gets frustrated, he takes the handbook once again and does some silent memorization.

Shenen: 'Solidarity is the most powerful thing, you should ask your friends for collaboration, start a new business, or study something together'

He: 'I don't have any friends. I have a cat'

Shenen: 'Are you jealous of someone?'

He: 'Yes, I am jealous of not one but many, I don't know what to do. Neither follow the crowd nor imitate others. What! Who wrote this handbook for you? cliché at its peak'

Shenen: 'Come on boy, please tell me the one good thing you are good at'

He: 'Sir, I know what to do if I was good at something. And I don't want to hear "No matter how much you earn or achieve from doing something you don't like, it won't be equal to a single penny you earn from doing something you like doing" this crap from your book. What am I supposed to buy with a penny? probably another penny! What kind of a helper are you? Atleast give me some money'

Shenen takes out his pocket watch (Twenty-two hours and twenty minutes remaining)

Shenen: 'Son, please meet me here, in the evening'

The shabby young man walks away; his face gives the impression that he will come back here in the evening.

Shenen is relieved, he keeps walking, finally takes a seat on the public bench. He notices a woman sitting on the other end of the bench, and she is crying. Shenen feels pity for her, he looks at the passerby people who don't care about her worry.

Shenen: 'Young lady, what's the matter?'

She: 'I am alone. I don't have anyone to hang out with. Nobody loves me. I am the most boring human being. And I don't know what went wrong with the past me and the present me'

Shenen: 'Are you unemployed?'

She: 'No, I have a good job that I achieved from years of hard work and dedication. But now, I have no one to celebrate my achievements with'

Shenen: 'Are you waiting for someone to join you here?'

She: 'How rude! Why did you insult me with my own sadness! I came here to find new friends, but no one cared to join me, then I decided to jump off that bridge, but I didn't have the courage to do that either' (weeps hard)

Shenen takes out his handbook, leaf through it, finds the section titled Alienation. But he is confused this time, he can't find the best response to the current situation. After a few minutes of silence, he found it

Shenen: 'Ok. Are you alone because you believe you are better than others and deserve the great? you haven't met anyone you are comfortable to hang out with? you hate human beings?'

She: 'I had friends. Am not a monster! And I don't believe I am better than others. Funny thing is, I believe I am the worst. And maybe it is the reason for me being alone. Nobody wants to hang out with a boring person!'

Shenen: 'Ok (flips to the next page) You don't want to co-operate with other people's weakness, and don't want to lose your time bettering them'

She: 'They don't like getting bettered. They have pride!'

Shenen: 'You believe you are stronger alone, and you don't want to show your neediness to meet someone'

She: 'They will take advantage of me, asking for a job, money, me. I don't want that kind of people in my life again!'

Shenen: 'You deserve better, and it is always better and a fact universally acknowledged that it is better to be alone than to be with incompatible people. You should not drink poison even if you are starving'

She: 'No, it's not good to be alone. I don't have anyone to talk about my life, and don't know what to do with my sad life. Perhaps I spent too much time for my career, but I had to because of the competition, my parents were worried'

Shenen: 'You are not alone; you have your parents. Chill with them, take care of them'

She: 'No, my parents died last year. I don't have any siblings either. You are a professional helper, help me'

Shenen again takes out his handbook, reads it a second time. He is sweating a little.

Shenen: 'Alienation rises from the slightest of indifference, because this difference can make anyone unkind'

She: 'I didn't ask you for a study guide. What's wrong with you? I didn't have spare time to spent with others. What should I do now?'

(silence)

Shenen: 'Marry someone. Have you tried that?'

She: 'Yes, but I couldn't find a good match! Give me that book!'

She grabbed the handbook from Shenen's hand and reads it for a few minutes.

She: 'What is this? It is one's choice to be alone or not! What is this explanation? Who are you?'

Shenen: 'I am Shenen, the kindest person you will ever meet. And I do agree that it is one's choice to be alone. Before you strike me, think about the fact that you hid yourself away from the people who loved you to study hard for your career stuff. And it was your choice'

She: 'What else should I have done? The competition is tough; I can't live without an income. It is a very common thing'

Shenen: 'You should have created a balance, see here (points to the page) Balance is key. You should have focused on your career along with keeping a good relationship with the people who cared for you. Make a schedule, stop wasting time scrolling through the internet, be open to your loved ones about your struggles, fears. See here (points to the page) plan your career early, never rush. It means that if you were planning your career in your teen years, you would not have to hide yourself away from the world around you. Competitions are only for the inadvertent ones who rush, not for the determined'

She: 'Stop explaining hypothetical facts. I am twenty-eight now, and I don't have a time travel thing. Now what?'

Shenen politely takes back his handbook, and requests her to meet him here in the evening. She agreed to his request, and she is somewhat excited for that. Shenen restarts his walk, and he is frustrated with the 'don't know what to do' situation that he has brought himself into. Shenen has decided to take shelter somewhere to avoid further interactions with random people. He gets into an abandoned house that is infested with creepers and dirt. Shenen takes out his pocket watch (Nineteen hours and thirty-seven minutes remaining) He cleans the bed and gets ready to take a good sleep, suddenly, Shenen starts dancing but his eyes are red and filled with tears.

Shenen storms outside, he keeps pressing the pocket watch hidden inside his pocket. The bizarre event came to a stop when he made his stop on the sidewalk, struggling to catch his breath. Turns out that the pocket watch has some magic powers to not let Shenen hide himself away from people. Out of nowhere, someone grabbed his left shoulder

He: 'Hey helper, come with me. No time to explain'

The mysterious man drags Shenen along with him. They made their stop in front of a two-story building.

He: 'Look mister helper, here take this money, hold this crowbar (takes a crowbar from the ground and gives it to Shenen, he then takes out a pistol, double checks the bullets) Now follow me and be prepared to swing it hard as you can'

Shenen: 'What is happening? What do you want? Is this your house? Robbers inside?'

He: 'This is my ex-girlfriend's house; she dumped me because I am not good for her. I want to teach her a lesson. The plan of action is, we enter, immobilize the inhabitants except her, and then I will teach her a lesson. Be careful not to let anyone call assistance. Let's move'

Shenen: 'What is wrong with you? She is right'

He: 'Hey, don't ask more questions. Just follow me, I will surrender after I teach her my lesson. If you don't come, I will shoot you dead now!'

Shenen: 'Why don't you write your lesson on a piece of paper and put it in this mailbox? Why are you planning to hurt others?'

He: (laughs) 'Stop joking man, come on, let's go inside. There is no car inside the garage, she may be alone. Today is my lucky day' (police siren sound) Shenen and him hide inside a bush nearby, Shenen takes out his handbook, and finds the section titled as Violence.

He: 'Ok, let's start, the police have gone'

Shenen: 'Let's wait a few minutes here, perhaps they have turned off the siren and will be secretly patrolling around... Are you going to rape her?'

He: 'Yes. I am going to teach her a lesson. You know how much I have spent to make her happy! She ended our relationship with Silence! and she is now preparing to marry someone who has a better job and richer than me. Yes, I am jobless, but Love does not need a job, it transcends money'

(Awkward silence)

Shenen: 'Ok. You know, punishments cannot reform people completely, but good education on ethical human values can. Human beings don't even have the authority to harm themselves, because they are the property of earth'

He: 'What! Are you a preacher or something? trying to find the damned to reverse them? And how am I a property of Earth? Show me your ID!' (aims the gun at Shenan's forehead)

Shenen: 'Calm down boy, let me explain... The birth and growth of each human being is centred on getting enough energy from food source. Earth provides food. And that's all I can find from this book. Anyway, it is the lazy mind that craves violence to satisfy a person's evil side, because it requires much work to satisfy their good side'

He: (laughs) 'What a joke! Tell me how I can satisfy my good side, I will try'

Shenen: 'For you to satisfy your good side, abandoning this mission of revenge is the number one thing to do. And you should pray for her happiness, be a good friend to her'

He: 'What! No, she is my only hope. I am thirty years old and have wasted all my years on her, I should have used it to better my body, my intellect. But I did all the work for my heart, and she betrayed me. Yes, I am not a good choice, but she is perfect for me. I can't get another woman to like me, look at me! Am spoiled'

Shenen: 'Wow. This handbook is good; each word you uttered now is in here. Look'

He grabs the handbook and silently reads the violence section.

He: 'Whoa! this is good. Parents should let men and women form friendship from their childhood time, and they will be given specific teachings about how to treat each other, about the boundaries they should follow. And create a comfortable humane ecosystem to let them openly discuss their secret fears of life. Never exploit someone's innocence! What is this book? Who wrote it – (flips the book both ways, stares at the only possible name to be considered as the author) – One? What's this?'

Shenen: 'One, the number?'

He: 'No, the statement "Never exploit someone's innocence" what is this supposed to mean?'

Shenen: 'Give me that (grabs the handbook back from him) let me take a look... Are you blind? A detailed description is right below the statement'

He: 'Yeah, I saw that. But am not in a mood to read it. Please read it for me. And nobody wants to read anymore'

Shenen: 'Fine. It means that you should not take advantage of a person's good side. I know you don't get it. Just imagine you and your ex-girlfriend, if she had a good side of taking care of animals, and you, knowing this, pretended to be an animal lover to gain this girl's interest, even though you would kill animals for fun. Get it?'

He: 'Do you know me? I feel insulted. Let me think... I lied to my ex-girlfriend about my parents getting divorced and neither one of them wanted me, because I knew that she was just two cliché lies away from building a pool of tears around her'

Shenen: 'That lie was something else. Good job. Are we done? Do you still want to revenge?'

He: 'Yes, she is my last shot. Come on man, let's go!'

Shenen and him slowly entered the house; the revenge boy's actions are clear to say that this is not his first time here. Shenen followed him patiently, the boy found her sleeping in her room. Shenen waited outside the room meanwhile the revenge boy carefully went near her and used a rolled-up towel to silence her. Shenen slowly sneaked behind the boy, the moment he climbed on top of her, Shenen pushed him off with sheer force, he crashed to the ground. Shenen picked up the girl and stormed out, locked the door. He made her call the police and ran away.

Shenen made his stop near the park, takes the pocket watch out (Sixteen hours and twenty-three minutes left) Darkness has started to make its presence here and there. Shenen is worried about how to fulfil his promises made to the lonely woman and the lazy unemployed man. He keeps studying the handbook, but his concentration gets broken by the sound of phone crashing. He runs his eyes around, finds a small boy aggressively throwing his smartphone to the ground, repeatedly. Shenen approaches the boy.

Shenen: 'What is the matter, little boy?'

Kid: 'I hate my life. This thing killed everything!'

Shenen takes out his handbook, leafs through it but couldn't find anything related to the subject.

Shenen: 'Who are you? Please explain, I can help'

Kid: 'I am Kevin, sixteen years old, student. I don't know what to do with my life. Nobody wants to guide me!'

Shenen: 'Relax son. Can you tell me what exactly you are feeling right now?'

Kid: 'I am feeling helpless, confused, depressed'

Shenen re-reads the handbook, the Kid is getting angry, Shenen finally finds the section titled Depression.

Shenen: 'It is one's own choice... Do you have a revengeful mind?'

Kid: (thinking deeply) 'Yes, I hate my parents. They don't love me. Every time I cried for something, they forced me to play in this thing! I don't like studying. My parents didn't teach me how to play cricket, how to ride a bicycle, where to find happiness. I have to internet my worries and am done with my internet life! I will not return to my house; this park is my new home'

Shenen: 'You just want an excuse to take your own life for granted. Also, an excuse to remain lazy. You should give value to the smallest things in your life'

Kid: 'What the! Stop reading from that book, you weirdo. This is real life; I have never experienced happiness'

Shenen: 'If home is not working for you, make school work for you. Make it your second home. Make new friends'

Kid: 'Easy for you, bookworm. My school is very strict, and they bully me every day for not doing homework, I don't have a peaceful home to study, and my parents don't care if I study or not, they send me school just to get rid of me. I heard them saying they want to be separated, and neither of them wants me. I will soon be sent to some boarding school. I am tired of getting abused. Please help me sir. Use your book'

Shenen: 'Don't worry son, please stay here, I will go and talk to your parents'

The Kid gave Shenen his address, he ran as fast as he could, checks his pocket watch (Ten hours and seven minutes remaining) finally found the right address, a two-story building. Shenen is welcomed inside by a middle-aged man, possibly the Kid's father. Shenen takes a seat.

Shenen: 'Where is Kevin's mother?'

Father: 'She is not here. I don't know where she is... you from school? Did he do any mischief?'

Shenen takes out his handbook, starts reading it silently. Meanwhile, Kevin's father has started scrolling on his phone.

Shenen: 'Getting away from one's responsibilities is like being a coward. You married, brought new life into this world, and it is your responsibility to raise him good. Stop wasting your limited time on earth fighting ego's. Why do you believe that you will be stronger alone? If she has a weakness, adjust. She will do that for you too'

Father: 'I am sorry! What?'

Shenen repeats everything he just said, thanks to his handbook.

Father: 'I don't have a weakness! She has a lot of them; it's like living with a donkey on two legs. I would have divorced her long ago if her family wasn't rich!'

Shenen: 'What about Kevin? He is depressed'

Father: 'What can I do? That's what schools are made for! Take him or give him to her. I don't care. He will also become a donkey like her mother. I don't want to raise a second Donkey anymore!'

Shenen rushed out of the building, ran faster to meet the Kid. Shenen's face clearly expresses his guilt for leaving the Kid alone in an open park, especially a depressed kid. Shenen's haste through the busy crowd made him clash with one of the pedestrians. They both fell, Shenen jumped up quickly, and helped the anonymous man back to his feet. The man offered a smile and walked away. Shenen is stunned by the man's response. Like us, he also expected a fight to happen. Shenen followed the man of forgiveness and found his shelter. Shenen's face lights up with happiness, and his previous expression of helplessness has disappeared.

Shenen ran back to the Kid, Kevin. Shenen paused for a minute, asked him to wait a little more, and then rushed to the main street. It is night, he takes out his pocket watch in mid-run (Six hours and twenty-five minutes remaining) (intense breathing) Shenen meets the unemployed man, and the lonely woman, he tells them to follow him. The trio ran quickly to meet the Kid. Shenen carries the Kid and continues his running marathon. He makes his stop in front of an entrance, drops Kevin, gently tells them to enter. Kevin the Kid, the lonely woman and the unemployed boy, they are all confused.

Woman: 'Why here? Mister helper, answer me!'

Shenen: 'Do you know this place?'

Boy: 'Yes, this is a monastery, a shelter for people who have devoted themselves fully to a deity'

Shenen meets a monk and asks him about the details. He replied that the monastery will provide food and shelter to its inhabitants.

Woman: 'Which deity do you serve here? Can I have the permission to go to work? How to become a server?'

Boy: 'Is there any income? Can I work for this institution?'

Kid: 'Thank you Sir, I will stay here. Please take me in, Master'

Monk: 'Don't worry, child, we are happy to take you in. Most of our new members are Kids and teenagers. We understand you. It is very common to get loose from the holds of the Soul, the ultimate Soul. Don't be worried, stay here and worship to tighten up your lost bonds with it. And you, young lady, don't worry about your work, go and work, come here whenever you want, we will always be here for you. And for you, young boy, you will receive blessings from the Soul of the Universe, to which we offer our efforts to'

Woman: 'That was the kindest stack of words I have ever heard from a real human being. I will work for this magical place, thank you master'

Boy: 'I thought to end my sad life once, and now I feel sorry for thinking like that. I am feeling internal bliss after a very long time, I am done with all the pretending. Thank you, sir, you are indeed a helper'

The lady, the boy and the Kid are pleased, and for the first time, an expression of happiness blooms on their face. They hug Shenen tightly for one whole minute and slowly walk into the main building. With Shenen, they explore the place. Finally, Shenen bids them farewell, and he is back in the streets, takes out his pocket watch (Forty-five minutes remaining) He finds a lonely bench near an electric lamppost, makes himself comfortable on it. He is relieved because the night has managed to get everyone back in their homes. After a few minutes, a mysterious man, wearing a superhero mask, sits near Shenen who instantly sensed his presence.

Him: 'Hey buddy, care to join a pleasure heist?'

Shenen: 'Where? What is that?'

Him: 'I have found a house where only two women live. Join me, and you can have one of – (gawk) (sound of heavy beating on flesh mixed with cries)

Ok. What happened there was that Shenen became enraged and he stabbed his handbook into the masked man's mouth; he fell to the ground gasping for air like a fish washed to the shore. Shenen then punched him hard, made him unconscious. Shenen accepts his defeat, kneels and closes his eyes. He waits for his punishment...

(intense breathing) Someone grabbed my shoulder from behind! I was frozen for a minute, slowly turned around to see an entity standing behind me. It has a face, but I don't know how to describe it or draw it. On further observation, I have realised that the entity does not have a face but reflects the objects standing in front of it. I saw my face on its face, and it is my first time seeing my face. I didn't know that I have a face. The entity starts talking, its voice is coming from within it like an inbuilt speaker.

Entity: 'You broke the laws of narration; you will be sent to the dungeon of nothingness for a hundred Galcade'

Me: 'What is a Galcade?'

Entity: 'You will find out, bye'

Me: 'Wait sir. Forgive me. I am not perfect'

Entity: 'Yes, I know. Enjoy your hundred Galcade'

Me: 'Who are you to punish me? The author? I was forced into this work, and did my best to make this not boring, and this is how you want to treat me? Am I not allowed to speak out my opinion? This book is a failure, just a waste of words, waste of Thirty thousand plus words!'

Entity: 'How dare you keep insulting my child! You know how much he suffered to create this work! You did good work last time, and that's why I made you narrate this work, the one mistake I have done'

Me: 'He? Abhinand? Is he the Author?'

Entity: 'Yes. Why are you laughing?'

Me: 'Only a fool would make him write, especially these kinds of special book. Who are you to trap me here and defend that irresponsible man? He is not super talented either'

Entity: 'I am the Soul of the Universe'

(silence)

Entity: 'I know he is not a super talented boy, but he possesses the courage to fully offer his mind to me, and that's all I wanted'

Me: 'Forgive me. I don't want to escape my punishment, but I still strongly believe that this book won't be enough to purify the evilness widespread across the whole Universe. This is not the first time, many writers have written books like this'

Entity: 'Yes, and they have made great changes to the world. I am not saying that this book will change the whole world into a better place, but it definitely helps the progression. And this progression is not solely depended on books; there are a lot of other factors helping the progress'

Me: 'There is this famous theory that the world will come to an end, and then the good phase will take birth'

Entity: 'Wisdom will erase the evils, and then the world will take its grateful rebirth'

Me: 'The Evils? Why gave them birth? All problems should have ended then?'

Entity: 'Evil is not born but transformed. At the beginning, there are only, too good and less good. Everything should stay in the middle that is 'Good'. If a person has no admiration for their self, they will be too good and humble. And if this person admires their self highly, they will be less good and will also be selfish and prideful. Instead, a person should admire their self but not highly'

Me: 'Ok, that's a good explanation. Just like, a person should eat food but not overeat, because they will then be called Gluttonous'

Entity: 'Exactly. Balance is key. When the time comes, the world will achieve balance. And this balance will be powerful enough to create a solid connection with the whole Universe to Me'

Me: 'Soul, I have a request for you. The reason behind the inclusion of fictional stories into the narration is my doing, not soul of Fiction. Please release it'

Entity: 'Ok. Release it'

The glass structure has disappeared; the bright light came closer to me and the entity. Soul of Fiction entered the mini building through the slightly opened door.

Entity: 'It is time for you to go. Learn more lessons from the dungeon of nothingness'

Me: 'What is it? Dungeon the building?'

Entity: 'It is a barren land of nothingness. No light, no structures, no sound, nothing. It helps everyone see their true self. Bye'

Me: (weeps) 'Bye...'

First Epilogue

"Good job, my boy, you do possess wisdom. Am so happy to see you progressed this much in your twenty-fifth year of birth. Now, tell me about the writing experience" Bright light spoke.

I am feeling a rebirth kind of experience. I have never thought of writing a philosophical work, I mean, I always believed that I wasn't matured enough to write it. Am happy that you and 'Someone' chose me to deliver this magnificent piece of written form. And... Oh, about my progression, I don't feel like I still have the potential to call myself worthy of someone to be called the 'Master' because I am sure that I was just a medium for you and the 'someone' to show the world what you two want the world to be.

"You are right and am glad you spelled it out yourself. To be called the 'Master' you have plenty more challenges to overcome, but you are on the right track. The lessons you have learned from this book, keep it to your heart. Never forget. And if you don't mind me asking, what is the new project you are working on?" Bright light spoke.

Well, I am currently working on a screenplay, for a movie. And am halfway there. But now that I have learned all these philosophical thoughts, I am going to reconsider my plan of action. I am just going to publish it as a book, so that everyone can enjoy it inside their mind, fly with the characters, take their time. And I will be releasing it in my native language also.

"Good, you have my blessing. What about this book? Any translation for this book?" Bright light asked.

Yes, I will translate this work also. And if you don't mind me asking, what is the urgent need of this work out in the market? You do know the fact that no one really cares about books anymore, right? So, what's up with all that?

"Why are you so negative, my dear? I know your loved ones have the same question for you. What else we should do? You give the answer" Bright light asked.

I apologise for my unwanted questions. It's just that I didn't get any validation from anyone on my published Trilogy of Novels. And people are getting lazier each day, they don't want to spend their time by doing something, like reading! They prefer watching movies, short videos etc. So, my point is, Books are history.

"Dear, let me ask this one question. What about you? Do you belong to this group of watchers?" Bright light asked.

Kind of, but am not fully into that, and I prefer books, they somewhat keep me away from the creepy internet world.

"See, the point is, the small percent is enough. And I know your next question will be, enough for what? The answer is, enough for the rise of the upcoming Era of Truth in which human values prosper, it will come after fifty plus years. And you are just a small piece in the puzzle. Overtime, the activities done by each piece will stick together and solve the ultimate puzzle to enter the sacred Era of Truth. Farewell, my boy, my blessings will be with you every time, Goodbye for now" Bright light replied, disappeared.

Second Epilogue

After hours of hard work, finally I have reached the place. The place where wisdom-filled air circulates around. The place most people call wretched. I have only one reason to be here, to meet him. To find him here, a vast land, is a difficult task. But I have received help from that invisible power that was with me the whole time of writing this work. I have found him; he is sitting like he knew I will come.

Me: 'Good morning, Master'

Master: 'Welcome writer. Need more stories? I know the book has ended. What is this visit for?'

Me: 'I am not feeling good, master. You have taught us all the sacred human values, but that is for the future era of truth, for the youths. My worry is about this era. What is the reason behind all this? Who's to blame? How much more to endure? Selfishness everywhere, Gender wars, try hard to show off, no guilt to betray and kill, the "not give a damn" groups, Alienation worship, Silence lovers, not heard of the emotion called Love! All taken for granted attitude!'

Master: 'Relax son, I understand your feeling. Worry is not the solution, must fight. It is the culture and society that determines how its citizens grow up. Analysing the problems mentioned by you, I think what's to blame is the Family-nation culture'

Me: 'What is that?'

Master: 'It is the worst state of living in which, human beings only think about themselves and their family'

Me: 'It is always like that, what's new?'

Master: 'I am talking about the decision of a family to turn itself into a Nation, fortifying themselves inside of it'

Me: 'It is true, master. But is this the only reason?'

Master: 'Let me clarify. The families turning into Nations has caused Unity to cease. Human being is a social creature. But this Family-nation culture fortifies them with its mighty shackles, turning humanity into caged animals'

Me: 'Who's to blame for all of this?'

Master: 'It is a part in the evolution theory. The multifamily culture has evolved into today's Family-nation culture because of, modernity's rapid inventions, and the increase of human beings' greed. Every Family-nation has its own rules, but common rules do exist. Son, do you know them?'

Me: 'Get a job, marry, become parents, raise children'

Master: 'Yes, the Family-nation culture does not allow people to use their creative mind. All seek the same fruit'

Me: 'Master, are you suggesting that we should ban family life? I don't understand'

Master: 'No, Family is important, but it should not turn itself into a Nation. The real issue starts before "getting a job" phase'

Me: 'Study years?'

Master: 'Yes, from the time Family-nation culture started, people believe that a person's life starts only after marriage, this belief destroyed their freedom, their creative skills, their loving soul'

Me: 'So, when is the time a person starts their life?'

Master: 'Right after their birth. Parents should give their children freedom, from their childhood years. Family-nation forts must be crashed down. Every age group needs their well-deserved freedom, and it should be given. If not, they will become selfish'

Me: 'But what if they misuse this freedom?'

Master: 'Then, they should be corrected. It is not ethical to restrict their freedom assuming that they will cause trouble. A Free mind is required to learn about their individual skills. And it is necessary to let them know more about the world. Books, newspaper, medias etc. are helpful for that. The more they know about the world, the more they understand their self. And, it is important to let them have the opportunity to discuss their knowledge with others, which will help them fill their knowledge gaps'

Me: 'That's what schools are for, right?'

Master: 'School life influences a person's social knowledge, helps them understand the common knowledge. But to enhance their individual knowledge, the after-school time is necessary. Let them interact with their loved ones. Schools have less freedom, but it's okay. The crucial thing is to not restrict their freedom outside school. The Family-nation culture destroyed their freedom; thus, every human being lived in such a culture, only works for their own Family-nation. All others will be considered their enemies...

(silence)

...Even at a younger age, they start their competitive run. They acquire the strength to defeat others by any evil means possible. Thus, an entire society fights each other for their own Family-nation fort. This selfish mind-set kills the creative side of theirs. Evil lurks in their "friendships" if any. They sacrifice their sacred essence gifted from God, by becoming warriors for their Family-nation rulers'

Me: 'Is there any solution to this state? To destroy this culture'

Master: 'The youths must unite and fight for their freedom. The police and Government should protect them. Youths must build friendships, respect friends, consider everyone equal. They must promote human values, say no to the written life schedule, embrace their own essence, and should help other captives. Love, formed out of respect is its purest form, such is not found in the toxic Family-nation culture'

Me: 'Master, what is the reason for the spike in violent crimes? Murders are normal nowadays. Any solution?'

Master: 'If a person commits a crime, it means that the culture in which that man belongs, has failed him. Just like we saw in the Keith's story part, it is the sins accumulated from an entire society that create criminals'

Me: 'Master, you are right. Every human being works for their own Family-nation, they don't care about their society or country. They work only for the money, not service. They feel happiness from other's demise. Instead of thinking about how to be happy themselves, they try-hard to make others believe that they are happy. The word "Kindness" is off the dictionary, they see everyone as their enemies. They live depressed, self-critiquing themselves, cursing themselves, and in the end, they blame their fate to find solace. Such a devastating time. Must endure it somehow. Thank you master'

www.ingramcontent.com/pod-product-compliance
Lightning Source LLC
Chambersburg PA
CBHW021550150726
47990CB00006B/2482